Implementing Therapy Dog Teams in Partnership with Best Practices for Schools

An Introduction for Volunteer Dog Handlers, Teachers, Counselors, and Administrators for Successful Integration Resulting in Researched Enhanced Student Well-Being

Gabrielle Matthew

Dedication

In recognition of the many professionals and volunteers who have paved the way before me, diligently making a profound and inspirational positive difference for the well-being of students. Thank you especially to those passionate participants sharing their stories and documenting successes to help facilitate and advocate for similar programs to be integrated into more and more educational settings.

During my research, I celebrated that some therapy dogs have become school mascots with their own hallway bulletin boards, yearbook pictures, and office plaques of recognition. Therapy dog teams can transform school communities in intangible ways that will never be measured, as well as by clear evidence from proven scientific research studies worldwide. The overall conclusion is that, in most cases, the tremendous benefits outweigh any concerns.

Contents

Recognition

Puppies are complicated and hard work. I must thank my husband for co-parenting and training Mac with me. He has also been very supportive of our therapy visits and helpful this summer at the library. He is my partner in every way.

Thanks to my mom, my greatest cheerleader, for always believing in my possibilities!

Also, Melissa has made the journey of therapy dog certification a wonderful experience and fun along the way! Ki, was there when I needed help with Mac while recovering from my broken leg.

The children in my neighborhood also helped train Mac to love his job and welcomed him to school on his first day!

Although my other dogs, Toby, Willa, and Sophie, have passed, I still remember them fondly for their unique personalities and the love they brought to our family.

Finally, thanks to our friends Craig and Nikki for sharing their happy home and two dogs, Jack (Mac's half-brother) and Jack's sister, Abby. We have made such beautiful memories!

Introduction

<u>Consider the possibilities:</u>

A cost-effective plan of action that might change how we think about education and well-being in our schools: picture the hallways buzzing with energy, classrooms filled with diverse, vibrant young minds, and amidst this, a pressing, ever-present challenge: our students' mental and emotional well-being.

Today, more than ever, our youth are facing unique pressures, from the fallout of the COVID-19 pandemic to rising rates of absenteeism, anxiety, depression, and loneliness. An increasing number of professionals are reporting data suggesting that children's mental health is in crisis.

Numerous studies have highlighted a significant decline in the mental health of children and adolescents. Here are some key statistics that illustrate this concerning trend:

<u>Prevalence of Mental Health Disorders:</u>

Globally, one in seven 10-19 year-olds experience a mental disorder, accounting for 13%of the global burden of disease in this age group, according to the World Health

Organization's November 17, 2021, report on the Mental Health of Adolescents. Also, suicide is the fourth leading cause of death among 15-29-year-olds. In addition, it is estimated that 1 in 7 (14%) 10-19-year-olds experience mental health conditions, yet these remain largely unrecognized and untreated.

A new study in 2023 indicated that one in five children and young people in England aged eight to twenty-five had a probable mental disorder. Also, 20.3% of eight to sixteen-year-olds had a probable mental disorder in 2023.

Nearly 20% of children and young people ages 3-17 in the United States have a mental, emotional, developmental, or behavioral disorder, and suicidal behaviors among high school students increased by more than 40% in the decade before 2019, as reported by the National Healthcare Quality and Disparities Report – NCBI Bookshelf 2022.

In 2018-2019, about 15% of adolescents ages 12-17 years in the United States had a major depressive episode, 37% had persistent feelings of sadness or hopelessness, and nearly 20% reported that they seriously considered suicide.

The Children's Society reports that 1 in 6 children aged 5-16 are likely to have a mental health problem, and the likelihood of young people having a mental health problem has increased by 50% in the last three years. Youth mental health hospitalizations increased by 124% from 2016 to 2022.

In 2021, 42% of U.S. high school students reported experiencing persistent feelings of sadness or hopelessness, a 50% increase from 2011. Furthermore, eating disorders in the U.S. have seen a dramatic rise, with 12.5% of 17 to 19-year-olds having an eating disorder in 2023, up from 0.8% in 2017.

<u>Impact of the COVID-19 Pandemic:</u>

The pandemic has exacerbated mental health issues, with the CDC noting a rise in poor mental health among high school students during this period.

The National Survey of Children's Health found that depression in children grew by 27% and anxiety by 29% over a five-year span, including the first year of the pandemic.

During the COVID-19 pandemic, more than 200,000 children in the United States lost a parent or primary caregiver, and many children are still grieving while facing additional challenges, such as moving to a different home or transferring to a new school.

The pandemic has also exacerbated existing disparities in mental health services, and there is a shortage of child and adolescent clinicians and school psychologists in the United States.

<u>Suicidal Thoughts and Behaviors:</u>

In the United States, nearly one in five high school students had seriously considered attempting suicide in the previous year, with 18% making a suicide plan and 10% attempting suicide.

The CDC's Youth Risk Behavior Survey showed that 18.8% of adolescents aged 12-17 years had seriously considered attempting suicide, and 8.9% had attempted suicide.

<u>Disparities and Risk Factors:</u>

Mental health issues are more prevalent among certain groups, with higher rates of anxiety and depression reported among female adolescents and LGBTQ+ youth.

Children living below 100% of the federal poverty level are more likely to have a mental, behavioral, or developmental disorder, with more than 1 in 5 affected.

<u>Access to Mental Health Services:</u>

Despite the high prevalence of mental health issues,

access to treatment remains a challenge. For instance, 34% of those referred to NHS services are not accepted into treatment. In 2021 and 2022, 20% of adolescents reported receiving mental health therapy, and 14% reported taking prescription medication.

There is a definite lag in finding specific facts because it takes time to research and document accurately; however, the following is another easy-to-understand reference: National Institute for Health Care Management (NIHCM).

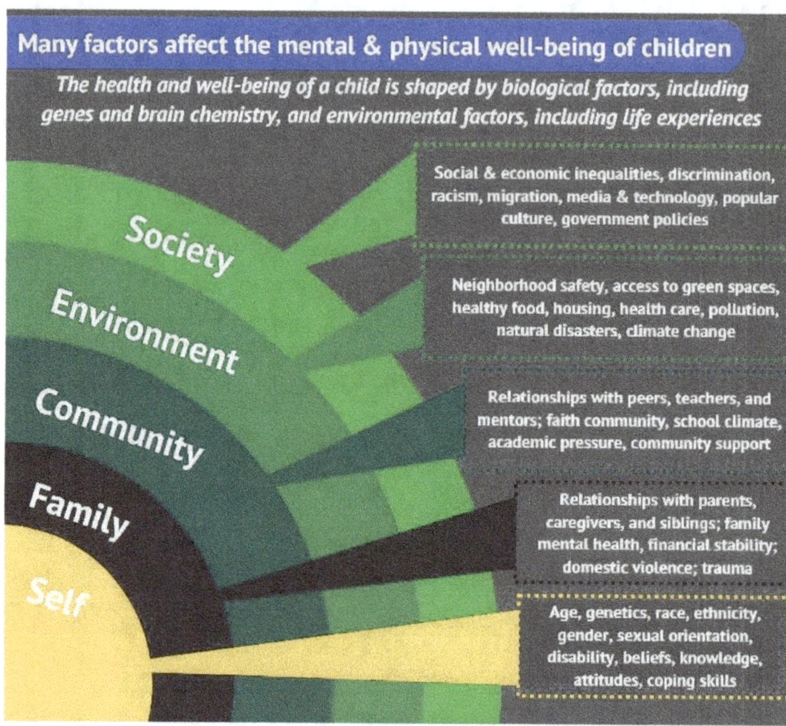

Many factors affect the mental & physical well-being of children
The health and well-being of a child is shaped by biological factors, including genes and brain chemistry, and environmental factors, including life experiences
Society
Environment
Community
Family
Self
Social & economic inequalities, discrimination, racism, migration, media & technology, popular culture, government policies
Neighborhood safety, access to green spaces, healthy food, housing, health care, pollution, natural disasters, climate change
Relationships with peers, teachers, and mentors; faith community, school climate, academic pressure, community support
Relationships with parents, caregivers, and siblings; family mental health, financial stability; domestic violence; trauma
Age, genetics, race, ethnicity, gender, sexual orientation, disability, beliefs, knowledge, attitudes, coping skills

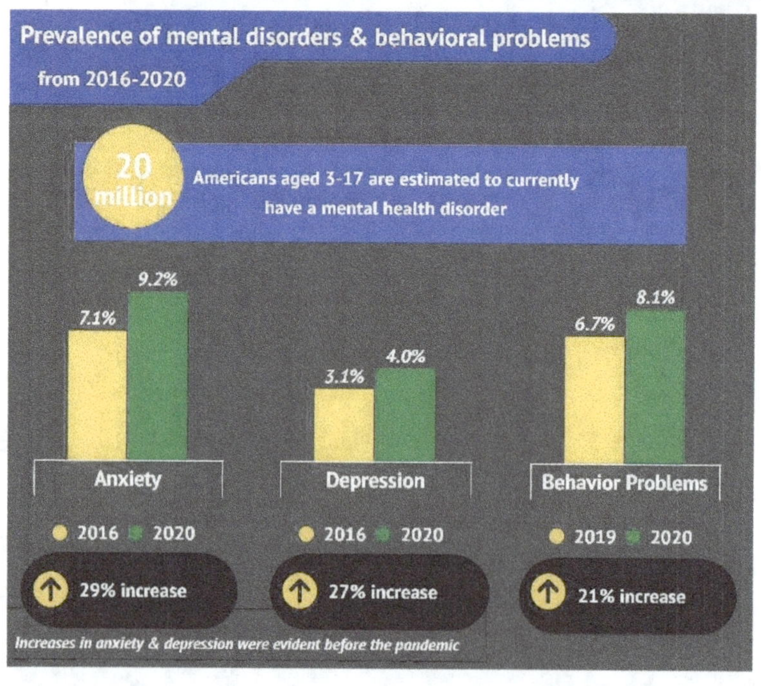

Prevalence of mental disorders & behavioral problems
from 2016-2020
20 million
Americans aged 3-17 are estimated to currently have a mental health disorder
9.2%
7.1%
3.1%
4.0%
6.7%
8.1%
Anxiety
Depression
Behavior Problems
2016
2020
2016
2020
2019
2020
29% increase
27% increase
21% increase
Increases in anxiety & depression were evident before the pandemic

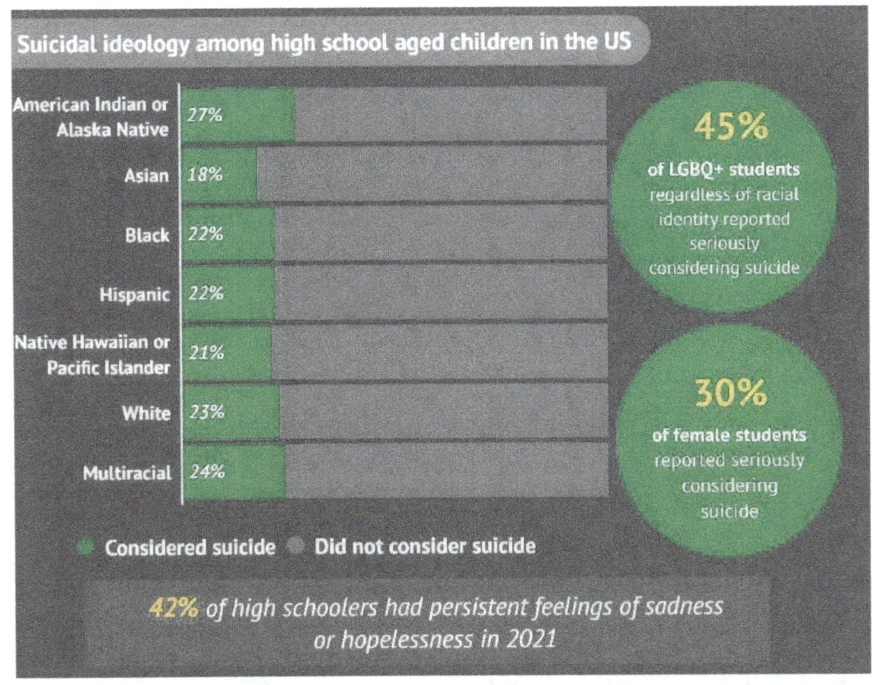

Suicidal ideology among high school aged children in the US
American Indian or Alaska Native 27%
Asian 18%
Black 22%
Hispanic 22%
Native Hawaiian or Pacific Islander 21%
White 23%
Multiracial 24%
Considered suicide
Did not consider suicide
45%
of LGBQ+ students regardless of racial identity reported seriously considering suicide
30%
of female students reported seriously considering suicide
42% of high schoolers had persistent feelings of sadness or hopelessness in 2021

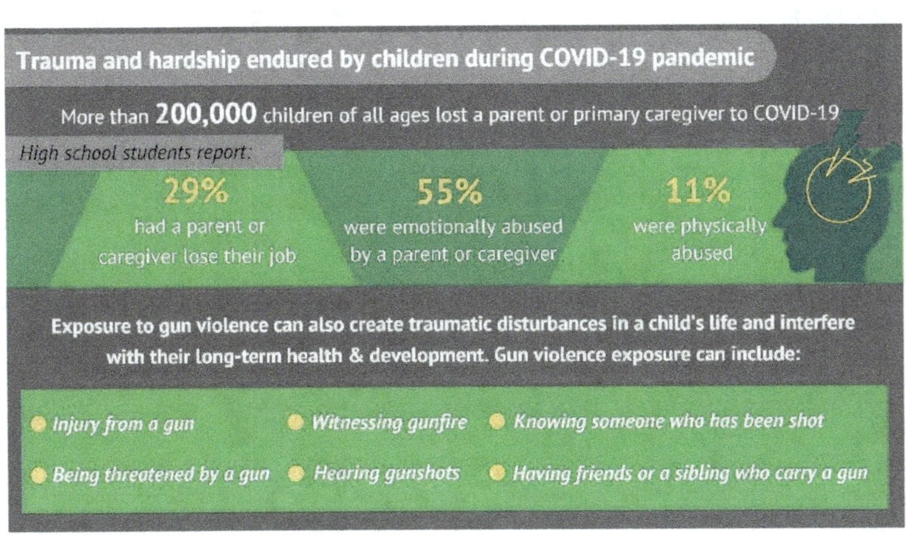

Trauma and hardship endured by children during COVID-19 pandemic
More than 200,000 children of all ages lost a parent or primary caregiver to COVID-19
High school students report:
29%
had a parent or caregiver lose their job
55%
were emotionally abused by a parent or caregiver
11%
were physically abused
Exposure to gun violence can also create traumatic disturbances in a child's life and interfere with their long-term health & development. Gun violence exposure can include:
Injury from a gun
Witnessing gunfire
Knowing someone who has been shot
Being threatened by a gun
Hearing gunshots
Having friends or a sibling who carry a gun

Promoting positive health and well-being for our children

Mental health and well-being

- **Build capacity** to better equip schools with psychologists to support student well-being onsite.

- **Bring mentors from the community** into schools, and making schools safer & more supportive for all types of students.

- **Utilize telehealth** during school hours for students who need extra support with one-on-one counseling.

- **Expand the mental health workforce** and early mental health screening through schools and pediatricians.

Physical health and vaccination uptake

- **Participate in 60 minutes of physical activity** every day.

- **Help schools implement a nutrition environment** that supports students in making healthy choices.

- **Improve messaging** from trusted messengers to increase vaccinations.

- **Implement school-located vaccination programs** and include incentives to increase vaccination.

Access to health care

- **Expand access to health coverage** for children and eliminate barriers to accessing coverage and care

Various factors contribute to the declining mental health of children and adolescents, including the widespread adoption of social media, long-term economic effects, worsening social contexts, and lower resilience among children resulting from changes in parenting practices.

These studies and corresponding statistics underscore the urgent need for innovative, compassionate solutions to support our students and to address this growing crisis. So, what can we do to help our students in need?

Enter the heartwarming, tail-wagging world of therapy dog teams. This growing movement is not just a trend but a testament to the power of human-animal bonds in creating positive change. Therapy dog teams, comprising well-trained dogs and their handlers (human partners), are making waves in educational settings by engaging students in activities that boost their mental health, enhance social skills, and even improve academic performance. A visiting therapy dog promotes interaction with other students and teachers. It has been empirically proven that therapy dogs stimulate memory and problem-solving skills.

Now, let me share a bit of my own story. My dog, Mac, and I have embarked on this incredible mission of becoming a certified therapy team. I'll never forget our first day walking into a school, the instant connection, and the sheer joy on the students' faces. It was a rewarding day that I had envisioned for several years. Mac and I have already experienced our profound impact on the children in our neighborhood. Also, the often private, keep-to-themselves neighbors of all ages started coming out to visit with Mac as we went on our regular walks. Mac's training began as a puppy, getting daily treats from the mailman while practicing manners. He quickly became a local celebrity among the neighbor kids, especially since they can give Mac commands he will follow for them. This, I have found, is very empowering for not only children, but also adults. There is no doubt that Mac has clearly illustrated the power of connection and community that a dog can bring into our lives.

This book was born out of my questions and challenges as Mac and I began navigating the world of therapy dog programs in schools. Specifically, before starting school visits, I needed to spend time and effort laying the groundwork so we could be successful in our efforts to aid students. I went to great lengths to research how other therapy teams around the country have organized themselves in partnership with schools. As a result, this book is meant to guide you to everything you need to know about integrating these incredible teams into educational settings. We'll cover the benefits, the research, the legalities, and the training, answering all those burning questions that I, too, once had. Additionally, this book will help clear roadblocks that get in the way of schools that desire to improve the quality of education by implementing therapy dog teams.

At the heart of this movement are volunteers like you and me, dedicated individuals passionate about making a difference. Despite the hurdles, such as navigating legal requirements/insurance issues and ensuring the safety of both students and dogs, this book aims to be your roadmap, offering practical solutions and step-by-step advice that will guide even those who are initially skeptical.

The ultimate goal is to enhance student well-being through the power of therapy dog partnerships. This book invites you to explore the incredible potential of volunteer therapy dog teams in schools. Together, we can start small, building confidence among all stakeholders and witness the joy and impact on the school communities.

So, let's set off on this adventure of discovery and transformation, envisioning the difference we can make in the lives of students and the broader school environments. Let's dive into the remarkable world of therapy dog teams in schools, documenting our successes and celebrating the connections that change lives. With good planning, all types and sizes of schools worldwide can effectively establish a flexible therapy dog program to meet each academic learning facility's unique goals.

Chapter 1. Defining Therapy Dog Partnerships

In the realm of canine companions, the distinction between service, emotional support, and therapy dogs often needs to be clarified. Yet, understanding this differentiation is the cornerstone of effectively integrating therapy dog teams into educational environments. The significant roles these animals play in human lives are not just a matter of semantics but are deeply rooted in the specific training they receive and their profound impacts on individuals and communities.

1.1 The Intricacies of Training: Delineating Service Dogs, Emotional Support Dogs, and Therapy Dogs

Service dogs are specifically trained to perform tasks that mitigate the disability of their handlers. Think of a service dog as an essential aid to a person with a physical disability, such as vision impairment, or a condition like epilepsy, where the dog is trained to alert for seizures. In contrast, emotional support dogs provide comfort and support through affection and companionship for an individual suffering from various mental and emotional conditions. Unlike their service counterparts, emotional support dogs are not trained for specific tasks related to a disability. Therefore, while the presence of an emotional support dog can be profoundly comforting, their role is not defined by task-oriented training.

Therapy dogs, the focus of our discourse, occupy a unique position. These dogs are trained to provide psychological or physiological therapy to individuals other than their handlers. Within the walls of a school, they become a source of comfort, a catalyst for social interactions, and a non-judgmental presence that can facilitate emotional or cognitive breakthroughs in students. While less task-specific than service dogs, their training is centered on cultivating an ability to interact amicably with various people in diverse settings, creating a climate of less stress.

The American Kennel Club's (AKC) Canine Good Citizen Class (CGC) is central to preparing a therapy dog. This program (a series of 6-8 class sessions) is designed to teach dogs the essentials of good manners and obedience through ten critical skills considered foundational for any therapy dog. These include accepting a friendly stranger, sitting politely for petting, and walking through a crowd. Beyond the basics, therapy dogs must undergo evaluations and background checks alongside their handlers to become certified. This rigorous preparation ensures that therapy dogs are well-behaved, adaptable, and capable of working in schools' dynamic and often unpredictable environments.

Several organizations in the United States offer certification for those seeking to formalize the status of their therapy dog team. Among these, Pet Partners, Alliance of Therapy Dogs, and Therapy Dogs International are notable. These certifications affirm the dog's and the handler's readiness, emphasizing the team aspect of therapy work. It is crucial to recognize that the certification is specific to the partnership between a handler and their dog, not a blanket endorsement of the handler to work with any therapy dog. This distinction underscores the importance of the bond and mutual understanding between the handler and their therapy dog, which is pivotal for the success of their interventions.

Having completed the AKC's CGC and evaluation testing, the therapy dog can navigate the school's lively environment, from the hallways' clamor to the excitement of young students eager to interact. The handler, certified alongside the dog, expertly manages the interactions, ensuring the dog remains calm and the students are engaged. The result is a harmonious session where students, typically reticent about participating, find confidence in the non-judgmental presence of the therapy dog. Here, the specialized training of the therapy dog and the insightful understanding of the handler converge to create an environment conducive to learning and emotional growth. Specific classroom or individual student goals can be developed based on each unique set of strengths of a particular therapy dog. Some younger dogs may be more appropriate for socialization skills, while older therapy dogs may be included in the classroom for students to gain non-judgmental experience reading aloud. It is a more than one-size-fits-all strategy that will be effective when trying to improve well-being. If carefully planned and thought through, there can be positive consequences for the school and the therapy dog handler and dog. Realizing this and wanting to avoid any setbacks from my hard work training Mac led me to seek resources, which, to be honest, were not so easy to find. To speed up the number of therapy dog partnerships in schools that can be successful, I gathered inspirational information and examples from multiple sources and put this book together.

The Road to Certification

In the spirit of providing practical guidance, below is an infographic that outlines the steps involved in becoming a certified therapy dog team:

- Step 1: Basic Obedience Training – Ensuring the dog masters simple commands.
- Step 2: Socialization – Exposing the dog to various environments and people.
- Step 3: Canine Good Citizen Certification – Completing the CGC Class and test.
- Step 4: Advanced Therapy Dog Training – Focusing on skills specific to therapy work.
- Step 5: Evaluation and Background Check – A certifying organization does this for the dog and handler.
- Step 6: Certification – Obtaining official recognition as a therapy dog team as evidenced by several

observations/evaluations in public facilities, such as commercial stores, nursing homes, hospitals, and other appropriate settings as deemed by the Therapy Dog Evaluators.

This structured pathway enhances the effectiveness of therapy dog teams and safeguards the safety of the students and educators they interact with. This preparation transforms therapy dogs into invaluable assets within educational settings, bridging gaps in communication, soothing anxieties, and facilitating a supportive atmosphere conducive to learning and emotional stability.

1.2 Socialization is Critical

Socialization emerges not merely as a step but as a cornerstone in preparing a therapy dog for the myriad environments and interactions it will face. The American Veterinary Society of Animal Behavior (AVSAB) clearly states in its position statement on puppy socialization that the first three months are a golden window for puppies to acquaint themselves with as many new beings and situations as possible. This practice lays a robust foundation, mitigating future fears and anxieties, thus preparing the dog for a lifetime of positive encounters.

The recent pandemic underscored the significance of socialization in a new light. As humans retreated into their homes, the rhythm of life altered dramatically for our canine companions. Puppies born during or just before the Covid-19 crisis found themselves in tranquil, human-centric worlds. The sudden absence of varied human interaction during crucial developmental phases left a void. Similarly, therapy dogs accustomed to regular interactions faced a stark shift. The return to normalcy, marked by the resumption of office work, introduced new challenges. Dogs, both young and old, experienced separation anxiety and a bewildering sense of isolation, underscoring the delicate relationship between early socialization and psychological characteristics.

While dog parks are often heralded as social havens, they warrant a cautious approach. The unpredictable nature of these environments, filled with unfamiliar dogs and people, can sometimes do more harm than good. A negative experience, such as an aggressive encounter, can imprint a lasting fear, making future interactions fraught with anxiety. This unpredictability makes controlled settings, where interactions can be monitored and managed, preferable for initial socialization efforts.

The value of playdates cannot be overstated in this context. Organizing meetings with "known" dogs and "trusted" owners provides a safe space for puppies to explore social cues and boundaries. These controlled interactions are instrumental in developing a well-rounded canine capable of navigating the complexities of human and animal relationships. Such early socialization efforts are comparable to laying the groundwork for a therapy dog's future effectiveness and resilience.

Doggie daycares, with their structured environments, offer another avenue for socialization. Here, dogs encounter a variety of breeds, temperaments, and play styles under the watchful eyes of professionals. Such experiences are invaluable, teaching dogs to adjust their behavior in response to different signals and situations. For a therapy dog, this ability to read and adapt is crucial. Whether comforting a grieving student or sitting patiently as children read aloud, the dog must discern and respond appropriately to the emotional states around them.

Moreover, therapy dogs benefit significantly from exposure to diverse settings beyond the canine world. Frequent visits to dog-friendly stores, banks, and cafes introduce them to a spectrum of human interactions and environmental stimuli. Each visit is a mini adventure, an opportunity to navigate new sounds, smells, and sights. This exposure is critical. Therapy dogs, after all, are not just any dog; they promote calmness in busy school hallways, a steady presence amid the chaos of recess, and a patient listener in the quiet of a library corner.

These experiences contribute to a therapy dog's repertoire, allowing them to remain unfazed by the unexpected and maintain their composure, regardless of the setting. The process is gradual, requiring patience, persistence, and well-thought-out planning by the handler. Yet, the rewards are exponentially powerful. A well-socialized therapy dog enriches the lives of those they interact with and experiences a more prosperous, more fulfilling life. In every wag of their tail and every gentle nuzzle, they exude confidence and comfort, a testament to the profound impact of comprehensive socialization and the human connections and bonds that are so powerful with dogs.

1.3 Understanding Dog Body Language

In the intricate dance of partnership between a therapy dog and their handler, a profound understanding of canine body language emerges as the linchpin of their mutual respect and situational awareness. A handler's capacity to read their dog's subtle cues, and vice versa, forms the bedrock upon which the efficacy of their interventions rests. This silent language, an unspoken dialogue of glances, postures, and movements, encodes the therapy dog's needs, preferences, and discomforts, serving as a compass guiding their interactions in the highly interactive ecosystem of a school.

A therapy dog, well-versed in human engagement, still relies on their handler to interpret their signals and advocate when the din of their environment becomes overwhelming or when an interaction veers towards stress rather than solace. The responsibility that falls upon the handler is not merely to guide but to listen, to perceive the whisper of a tucked tail or the subtle shift of ears laid back as precise indicators of the dog's state of mind. This dialogue, though silent, is dynamic, an ongoing exchange that demands attentiveness and sensitivity from the handler.

For those embarking on this path, the literature offers rich resources that delve into the intricacies of canine communication. Patricia McConnell's "The Other End of the Leash" stands as a seminal work, bridging the gap between human and canine perspectives, offering readers a lens through which to decode the language of dogs. With her background in animal behavior, McConnell elucidates the often misinterpreted signals dogs use to express anxiety, excitement, or contentment. Her insights give handlers the tools to navigate the complexities of canine emotions, fostering a deeper connection and understanding between them and their therapy dogs.

Turid Rugaas' "On Talking Terms With Dogs: Calming Signals" complements McConnell's work, focusing on calming signals, a repertoire of behaviors dogs employ to avoid conflict and express discomfort or anxiety. Rugaas, through her detailed observations, catalogs these signals, such as yawning, licking lips, or turning away, as dogs use mechanisms to self-soothe and signal to others, including their handlers, their need for space, or a change in interaction. For a therapy dog handler, recognizing these signals is crucial. It enables them to intervene proactively, ensuring that the dog does not feel trapped or overwhelmed, conditions under which their ability to provide comfort and support could be compromised.

The imperative for handlers to master this language of cues and signals cannot be overstated. Within a school's dynamic and unpredictable environment, where children's reactions can be both boisterous and unexpected, the handler's ability to interpret their therapy dog's communications ensures the dog's well-being and the students' safety. An adept handler, attuned to their dog's language, can discern when a break is needed, when to step back from an interaction that is escalating beyond comfort, and when their dog is fully engaged and responsive. This level of attunement creates a safe, effective, and mutually beneficial environment for the dog, the students, and the faculty they are there to support.

Moreover, this understanding extends beyond the immediate interactions. It informs the scheduling of visits, the design of activities, and even the selection of settings within the school that best suit the dog's temperament and communication style. It is a dynamic process, a continuous learning journey for the handler, as each dog possesses a unique set of signals and preferences. For this book, I do not address dogs who stay all day at school with handlers who are staff members. My experience is with a young dog, who I know would need to be more experienced to handle longer than a few hours of visitation at a time. One of the most important lessons

I do <u>not</u> wish to learn the hard way is to recognize when to leave a session, even if it isn't during the planned ending time. Just remember, as a handler, "Know When to Go."

In practice, this deep understanding of canine body language transforms the therapy dog program from a simple presence in the school to a sophisticated emotional and educational support tool. A therapy dog whose signals of discomfort are promptly recognized and addressed remains a calm, steady presence, a source of comfort for students. The dog's ability to stay engaged, to offer solace or a playful reprieve, hinges on the handler's skill in reading and responding to its nonverbal cues.

This partnership, underpinned by mutual respect and a shared language of subtle cues, becomes a model for empathy and communication within the school. Students, observing the interactions between the handler and the therapy dog, learn the value of attentiveness, respecting boundaries, and the unspoken bonds that can form between species. It is an education not just in reading or math but in life, in how we communicate, care for, and understand one another.

One example of why it is essential to lay a proper foundation for implementing therapy dog partnerships in schools is to imagine a big busy school in the middle of the day with students changing classes, going to lunch, coming back from outside recess; in other words, lots of activity in the halls and most common areas. If this school has never hosted a therapy dog team, it is only natural for the students we pass by to want to approach Mac randomly. Since we travel to many parts of the school, even though we may only visit one or two classrooms, preparing the entire student body beforehand is a good idea, as this will be new to everyone. Still, interactions should be handled in a particular manner. For example, students and staff should be expected to ask permission to approach or pet therapy dogs in schools. Also, immense crowding around the dogs is discouraged to keep them from becoming overwhelmed.

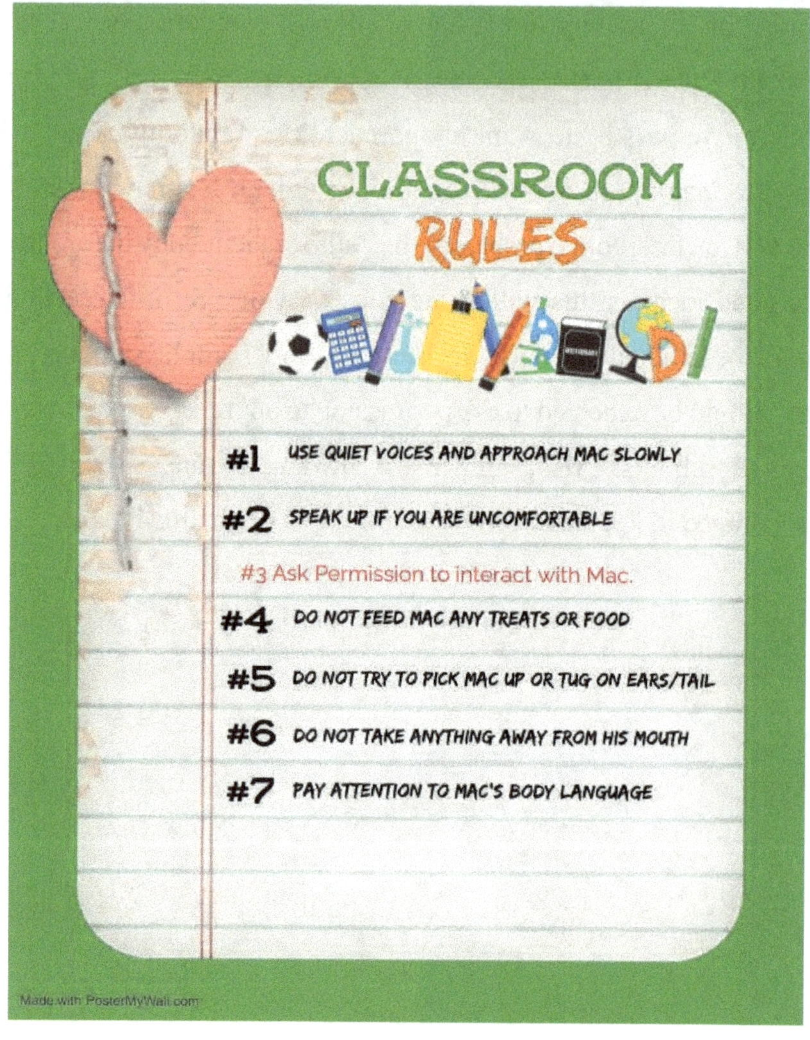

I prepared a simple set of Classroom Rules regarding appropriate ways to interact with Mac. With the assistance of the teachers, a discussion with the students in the classroom took place before we even entered the room. The entire introductory session consisted of demonstrating and reviewing these guidelines with the help of two neighbor children, who had practiced with Mac specifically for his preparation to visit schools. In addition, upon the advice of a trainer, Mac had his snuffle mat to serve as a 'safe' space for him to retreat to when tired, confused, or uncomfortable. The students learn to respect Mac's personal space as a sign to disengage and take a break. This also becomes a powerful lesson for students who may have issues with self-regulation. In case you don't already know, using snuffle mats offers numerous benefits, both for their physical and mental well-being. Snuffle mats are interactive pallets with multiple layers designed to mimic the natural foraging and scavenging behavior, which is actually very calming for dogs. The act of searching for food in the mat taps into their natural instincts and can help alleviate stress and anxiety.

Ultimately, the journey of a therapy dog team in a school setting becomes one of mutual growth, an intertwining path where each step strengthens the bond, enhances the understanding, and deepens the impact of their work. The silent conversations between handler and dog echo through the halls, a testament to the power of listening, understanding, and responding with empathy. In this exchange of silent dialogue, the therapy dog team finds its rhythm, navigating the complexities of school environments with grace and offering solace, support, and understanding to all they encounter.

Chapter 2. Discovering Purpose Through Partnership

In a world where the quest for meaning often leads us through a labyrinth of fleeting pursuits, the partnership between a therapy dog and their handler emerges as an experience of genuine fulfillment. This alliance, rooted in mutual respect and a shared mission, offers more than just companionship; it provides a profound sense of purpose that ripples through communities, transforming lives in educational settings. Here, amid the laughter and learning of students, therapy dog teams find a unique calling, blending skills, empathy, and an unwavering dedication to the well-being of others.

2.1 Sense of Purpose

Schools are full of diverse talents, backgrounds, and aspirations. When therapy dog handlers bring their canine partners into this vibrant atmosphere, they do not merely fill a role; they infuse it with their expertise and passion. For retired educators who chose to continue to volunteer, the school setting is familiar ground, yet introducing a therapy dog opens new avenues for engagement. Their deep understanding of pedagogy and classroom dynamics, combined with the therapeutic presence of their dogs, creates an enriched learning environment where emotional and educational growth flourish side by side.

Likewise, psychologists transitioning into handlers find their expertise in human behavior and mental health offers invaluable insights into the intricate interactions between students and therapy dogs. Mac and I benefited tremendously from the school psychologist being present when we started visiting at school. She already knew the students we were assigned to visit and helped prepare us for any possible complications. Her expertise helped structure these encounters with a keen eye for the subtle impacts, fostering an atmosphere where every pat and wag can contribute to a student's emotional toolkit. This cross-pollination of skills and the therapy dog's innate empathy merge into a powerful force for positive change within the school community.

At the heart of this partnership lies an unbreakable bond between handler and dog, a connection that transcends the ordinary relationship between pet and owner. Together, they navigate the bustling corridors and classrooms, a united front ready to lend support, offer comfort, and celebrate successes. This bond is the engine of their shared purpose, driving them to make a difference in students' lives. It's a reminder that at the core of every meaningful endeavor lies a connection, a mutual understanding that what they do matters.

Empowerment blooms from this sense of purpose. Handlers, equipped with their unique skills and the unwavering support of their canine partners, find themselves capable of touching lives in ways they never imagined. They witness firsthand the transformative power of their work, from the shy student who finds their voice in the presence of a therapy dog to the anxious child who discovers calm in gentle strokes of fur. These moments of impact are affirmations of their role, fueling their commitment and empowering them to push boundaries, innovate, and expand the reach of their programs. In the classroom that Mac and I visited, for instance, one young boy who had a phobia of dogs became comfortable with Mac quickly within the first two sessions.

The core components - the handler, the therapy dog, the faculty, and the students – all influence flow among them. Each element is linked to specific outcomes, such as improved student well-being, enhanced learning environments, and the personal growth of handlers, showcasing the holistic impact of these partnerships. The interconnectedness and the wide-reaching effects of integrating therapy dogs into educational settings are very moving and powerful.

In every interaction, every planned activity, and every spontaneous encounter, therapy dog teams are not just participants in the school's daily life; they are catalysts for a deeper understanding of empathy, resilience, and community. Through their dedication and the unique blend of skills and warmth they bring, schools become more than places of learning; they transform into havens of emotional support and personal development.

As a visit unfolds and a therapy dog gently nudges a hesitant student towards a book, the scene captures the essence of this purpose-driven partnership. In this moment, the handler's expertise, the dog's intuitive comfort, and the student's budding confidence converge, weaving a story of impact that extends far beyond the confines of the classroom. In these interactions, the value of therapy dog teams is revealed in their joy and comfort and the lasting changes they inspire within the school community.

2.2 Therapy Dogs Enjoy the Stimulation and Socialization of Their Jobs

Therapy dogs find a dynamic environment ripe for exploration and engagement within the school buildings. Tailored to thrive amidst various stimuli, these dogs possess temperaments that adapt to and flourish within the vibrant corridors and classrooms. Their innate curiosity and love for interaction make them perfect companions, eager to discover new faces and experiences daily. This zest for life, combined with a calm and gentle demeanor, enables them to navigate the diverse demands of a school setting with ease and enthusiasm. As some people have simplified it: "Therapy Dogs Spread Love."

Matching the distinct personalities and capabilities of therapy dogs with the specific needs of a school requires a sophisticated understanding of both. A dog that exudes boundless energy and joy might be the perfect catalyst for encouraging physical activity among students, transforming a simple game of catch into a lively and inclusive playground event. Conversely, a dog with a serene and patient presence becomes a comforting confidant for students navigating the complexities of stress and anxiety, offering silent support through their steady companionship. This strategic alignment ensures that the unique qualities of each therapy dog are maximized, fostering meaningful interactions that resonate with students and staff alike.

Implementing a healthy schedule for therapy dogs is paramount to maintaining their love of their job and ensuring the longevity of their service. Recognizing the signs of fatigue and overstimulation is crucial, as it allows handlers to provide necessary breaks and downtime, ensuring that the dogs remain at their best. Regular intervals of rest amidst the day's activities, coupled with a predictable routine, help preserve the dog's mental and physical health. Moreover, continuing socialization by engaging in activities outside the school environment is still crucial. In many locations, stores such as Lowes, Home Goods, and T.J. Maxx welcome dogs. This continuous interaction with new people, places, and situations contributes to their balance. Remembering to take days off is also important, allowing the dogs to recharge and return to their roles with renewed vigor and enthusiasm.

The symbiotic relationship between therapy dogs and their

handlers is pivotal in successfully integrating these teams into schools. It is a partnership founded on mutual respect, understanding, and a shared commitment to enriching the educational experience. With their insight into the dogs' personalities and needs, handlers serve as the linchpin, facilitating interactions that respect the dogs' boundaries while maximizing their impact on the student body. This delicate balance ensures that the therapy dogs' work remains a source of joy and fulfillment rather than a burden.

In essence, therapy dogs bring a multi-dimensional contribution to the educational setting, one that transcends the mere presence of a friendly animal. They introduce an element of spontaneity and warmth that can transform the school atmosphere, breaking down barriers and nurturing a culture of empathy and inclusivity. Their daily interactions teach invaluable life lessons on kindness, responsibility, emotional stability, and satisfaction. These lessons leave a lasting imprint on the hearts and minds of students, shaping their perspectives and attitudes in profound ways.

A sense of accomplishment fills the air as a school visit ends, and the therapy dogs complete their session. Each wagging tail and gentle nuzzle contributed to a larger narrative that speaks to the power of connection and the transformative impact of therapy dogs in educational environments. The day's experiences, rich in learning and emotional growth, underscore these dogs' irreplaceable role in fostering a supportive and compassionate school community.

Reflecting on the journey thus far, it becomes evident that integrating therapy dogs into schools is not merely an addition to the educational toolkit but a fundamental shift towards a more holistic approach to learning and well-being. Their presence illuminates the interconnectivity of academic success and emotional health, advocating for a learning environment where students are nurtured in mind, body, and spirit. As we move forward, the insights gained from this chapter lay the groundwork for deeper exploration into the implementation and management of therapy dog programs, guiding us toward strategies that ensure their success and sustainability. The path ahead is filled with potential, promising continued growth and enrichment for students, staff, and therapy dogs as we strive to create learning spaces that embrace the full spectrum of human and canine potential.

Chapter 3. Real-Life Examples: The Application of Therapy Dog Teams in Schools

The most inspiring implementation of a therapy dog team in a school I have come across, was while virtually attending AAAIP's mini-conference on Feb 29, 2024: Therapy Animals in Schools-Addressing the Most Common Questions. One presenter, Dr. Barbara Vokatis, summarized interventions for student's writing and literacy labs. Her experiences stand out regarding therapy dogs' powerful impact and are a direct example of improving academic learning through specialized curriculum applications. Students who were reticent to write over time began to envision themselves as authors. The power of visualization techniques added to the holistic approach to learning and growing. Dr. Vokatis collaborated with the classroom teacher specifically to achieve targeted outcomes. The complete workshop video, I believe, is on YouTube.

Dr. Vokatis and many other handlers involved in schools have also written books suited for students based on their therapy dogs' real-life experiences in schools. These books are perfect icebreakers for new therapy dog teams to read to students during the beginning of new student sessions.

Another example of an amazing therapy dog team, who now has formed the non-profit You're Not Alone, is best appreciated by watching the Minnesota CBS TV news feature on YouTube.

https://www.youtube.com/watch?v=u6Qm3dV8Bdc

This mission emphasizes utilizing therapy dog teams as pseudo-counselors in conjunction with school staff. The founder, Amy, is extremely dedicated and has been successful in expanding middle school programs in her state. This video is perhaps the most powerful documentation of how amazing therapy dog teams can transform students' well-being. Hopefully, more videos like this will be used to further the cause of school therapy dog teams.

Later chapters will include more real-life successful therapy dog implementations in schools; however, I wish to emphasize how many different academic and sociological student goals can be practically achieved with good planning and collaboration with school professionals.

Chapter 4. Tracing the Threads of Compassion

Integrating therapy dogs into educational settings took time. It results from decades of evolving practice, countless instances of human and canine interactions that have gradually shaped the landscape of learning environments. This chapter delves into the origins and transformation of therapy dog programs in schools, shedding light on the pioneering efforts that paved the way and examining how different cultures across the globe have tailored these programs to meet their unique educational needs.

4.1 Historical Overview

Using animals for therapeutic purposes can be traced back to ancient civilizations, but the formal incorporation of therapy dogs into educational environments is a relatively recent development. It emerged from a broader understanding of animal-assisted therapy (AAT), which gained prominence in the 20th century thanks to the work of pioneers such as Boris Levinson. Levinson, a child psychologist, accidentally discovered the therapeutic potential of his dog, Jingles, during sessions with an autistic child and introduced the concept of integrating therapy dogs into school settings to the American Psychological Association, which since then has gained prominence.

As AAT gained traction, educators began to explore the potential benefits of therapy dogs in schools. The initial forays were modest, often initiated by teachers who witnessed firsthand their pets' calming effect on students. These early adopters navigated a landscape devoid of formal guidelines, relying on intuition and observation to integrate therapy dogs into their classrooms. The outcomes, marked by anecdotal evidence of improved student well-being and engagement, fueled a growing interest in formalizing therapy dog programs within educational settings.

4.2 Evolution of Practice

Over time, the practices surrounding using therapy dogs in schools have undergone significant refinement. What began as informal visits has evolved into structured programs designed to meet specific educational and therapeutic objectives. This evolution has been driven by a confluence of factors, including advancements in research on human-animal interactions, the development of certification standards for therapy dogs, and a growing recognition of the varying needs of students.

In the early stages, the focus was primarily on the dog's presence as a novel stimulus, believed to foster a more relaxed and conducive learning environment. However, as understanding deepened, the role of therapy dogs expanded. They began to be seen as passive participants and active facilitators of learning and emotional support. This shift prompted a more strategic approach to their integration, with activities tailored to harness the specific benefits of therapy dog interactions, such as reading programs designed to boost confidence and literacy skills among students.

4.3 Pioneering Programs

The concept of integrating therapy dogs into school settings has gained prominence over the years. Let's explore some key milestones in the development of therapy dog programs in U.S. schools:

1. Pet Partners (formerly Delta Society):

    - Founded in 1977, Pet Partners played a pioneering role in promoting animal-assisted activities and therapy.

2. B.F. Kitchen Elementary School's Comprehensive Program:

    - In Loveland, Colorado, a therapy dog program at B.F. Kitchen Elementary was developed.
    - This program was established after the participants participated in a research study conducted by the Human-Animal Bond in Colorado (HABIC).
    - The study explored the emotional availability of students when working with a therapy dog team.
    - Notably, the therapy dog team's presence led to a decrease in office referrals and an increase in empathy among students.
    - Over the past decade, the program has expanded to

include a thriving volunteer team with numerous active therapy dogs.

- More than 12,000 positive interactions have occurred between students and these furry companions.
- The program's success has also led to the creation of a website and a social media group dedicated to sharing information about school therapy dogs.

3. Yale Law School's Monty:
- Over ten years ago, Yale Law School introduced General Montgomery (Monty) as their therapy dog.
- Monty's role was to help students manage stress levels, particularly during their initial years at law school. His presence in the school's library provided comfort and support to students, demonstrating the positive impact of therapy dogs on mental well-being.

In summary, therapy dog programs have evolved significantly, benefiting students by reducing stress, fostering empathy, and creating positive connections within schools. These furry companions play a vital role in promoting emotional health and enhancing the overall school experience. ⍰

4.4 Global Perspective

Adopting therapy dog programs in schools is not confined to any region or culture. Educators worldwide, from the United States to Japan, Australia, and Europe, have embraced the potential of therapy dogs, all interested in enhancing the learning experience. However, the approach and emphasis can vary significantly from one country to another, influenced by cultural attitudes toward dogs, educational philosophies, and regulatory environments.

In some European countries, therapy dog programs have been integrated into comprehensive well-being initiatives encompassing students and staff. These programs often emphasize the holistic benefits of therapy dog interactions, including stress reduction and emotional regulation, aligning with broader educational goals of fostering well-rounded, resilient individuals.

Conversely, in Japan, where space constraints and cultural norms present unique challenges, therapy dog programs tend to be more focused and event-driven. Schools might organize specific days when therapy dogs are brought in to interact with students, focusing on relieving academic pressures and fostering social connections.

To illustrate the international connection and bonding between humans and canines, I highly recommend watching the documentary- We Don't Deserve Dogs. Although this production does not explicitly address schools, it is compelling to remember that the bonding evidence between humans and dogs is universal.

https://www.wedontdeservedogs.com/

The trajectory of therapy dog programs in educational settings is a testament to the enduring bond between humans and dogs. This relationship transcends mere companionship to catalyze growth, understanding, and healing. As we trace the history and evolution of these programs, we uncover a narrative of progress, challenges, and relentless pursuit of a shared goal: to enrich students' educational journey through the compassionate presence of therapy dogs. The old saying, "Man's Best Friend," resonates worldwide.

Chapter 5. Decoding the Science: How Therapy Dogs Aid Learning and Well-Being

There is so much evidence about the multiple advantages and benefits that therapy dog teams can bring to the lives of students and staff in educational settings.

5.1 Neurological Impact

The interaction between students and therapy dogs instigates a cascade of neurochemical events within the brain, fundamentally altering the body's stress response and enhancing cognitive functions crucial for learning. The mere act of stroking a dog can trigger the release of oxytocin, commonly dubbed the 'love hormone,' which fosters feelings of trust and relaxation. This hormonal surge is critical in dampening the fight-or-flight response, mediated by the amygdala, and promoting a calm readiness conducive to learning. Concurrently, interactions with therapy dogs have been shown to precipitate a decline in cortisol levels, the primary stress hormone, further facilitating an environment where attention spans are lengthened, and the absorption of new information is optimized. This neurochemical transformation, engendered by the presence of therapy dogs, creates a physiological state that supports academic engagement and retention, underscoring the profound interconnectedness of emotional well-being and cognitive performance.

5.2 Emotional Support

The role of therapy dogs in providing emotional support transcends the typical boundaries of human interactions, offering a unique avenue for expressing and understanding emotions in a school setting. These canine companions serve as non-judgmental, accepting entities around whom students feel a sense of safety and openness. A therapy dog's unconditional acceptance is devoid of the complexities often inherent in human relationships, making these animals ideal candidates for students navigating the turbulent waters of growing up. This emotional bond mitigates feelings of loneliness and anxiety and cultivates a sense of empathy and compassion within students. Through their interactions with therapy dogs, students learn to recognize and respect vulnerability in themselves and others, fostering a classroom environment that champions emotional intelligence alongside academic achievement. This heightened emotional awareness contributes to a more cohesive and supportive social environment within the school, where students feel valued and understood, significantly enhancing their engagement and participation in learning activities.

5.3 Behavioral Improvements

Documented observations and studies delineate a noticeable decline in behavioral issues among students exposed to therapy dog programs. The presence of these animals within educational settings acts as a natural modulator of student conduct, encouraging self-regulation and positive social interactions. Therapy dogs serve as catalysts for cooperation and kindness, traits that are reinforced through structured activities that promote group participation and individual accountability. For instance, students tasked with caring for a therapy dog during its visit learn the importance of responsibility, patience, and gentleness—skills that translate into broader behavioral improvements outside the context of the therapy dog program. These shifts in student behavior contribute to a more harmonious classroom dynamic and alleviate the pressures on educators, enabling a focus on pedagogical goals rather than disciplinary measures. The cumulative effect of these behavioral adjustments is a learning environment that is both more productive and more inclusive, characterized by mutual respect and a shared sense of purpose.

5.4 Attendance and Engagement

Introducing therapy dogs into schools has a marked influence on student attendance and engagement, aspects critical to the educational success of any institution. The anticipation of interacting with a therapy dog provides a compelling motivation for students to attend school, particularly for those who might otherwise feel disengaged from the educational process. This effect is particularly pronounced in students who face challenges in their learning journey, whether due to emotional difficulties, social isolation, or learning disabilities. The non-threatening presence of a therapy dog offers a bridge to re-engagement, transforming the school space into one of joy and belonging. Furthermore, therapy dogs act as living, breathing focal points of interest and curiosity, stimulating discussions and activities that pique students' interest in various subjects. This heightened engagement enriches the educational experience and fosters a deeper connection between students and their learning environment, driving academic curiosity and achievement. Therapy dogs contribute to a positive cycle of attendance and engagement by being present, laying the groundwork for a more fulfilling and practical educational experience.

5.5 Diverse Settings, Diverse Impacts: Therapy Dogs Across School Environments

<u>Elementary Schools</u>

In elementary school's vibrant, often chaotic world, therapy dogs emerge as anchors of emotional stability. Here, young learners, still at the cusp of developing their social and emotional competencies, encounter these canine companions as more than mere pets; they become co-educators, silent guides through the complexities of growing up. The tactile stimulus of a soft fur coat under small, tentative hands soothes and stimulates neural pathways conducive to learning, making therapy dogs invaluable in these formative years. Activities designed around these canine companions, from reading sessions where a dog's patient presence encourages hesitant readers to articulate words more confidently to science lessons that explore animal care, imbue the curriculum with an experiential richness that textbooks alone cannot provide. For children navigating the challenges of social integration and the development of empathy, the non-verbal communication and unconditional acceptance offered by therapy dogs serve as critical lessons in understanding and kindness.

Secondary Schools

As students transition into the tumultuous phase of adolescence, marked by a quest for identity and a heightened sensitivity to social dynamics, therapy dogs in secondary schools offer a unique form of support. The pressures of academic performance, combined with the complex dance of peer relationships, often culminate in a milieu rife with stress and anxiety. With their intuitive sense of connection, therapy dogs provide a respite, a momentary pause from the relentless pace of teenage life. Their presence in classrooms and common areas becomes a subtle yet powerful intervention that alleviates stress, encourages conversation, and fosters a sense of belonging. For students wrestling with the isolation that sometimes accompanies this stage of development, a therapy dog's nonjudgmental companionship can be a lifeline, offering solace and a reminder of the joy in simple connection. In fact, introducing therapy dogs into health and wellness programs underscores the school's commitment to holistic education, which values mental health as equally as academic achievement.

<u>High Schools, Colleges, and Universities and After School Programs</u>

In the more mature echelons of the educational spectrum, where academic and future career anxieties intensify, therapy dogs contribute significantly to reducing stress and enhancing student engagement. Their integration into high schools, colleges, and universities—environments often characterized by competitive pressures and looming life decisions—introduces an element of fun and comfort. Programs tailored for these settings, such as the University of Rochester's 'Paws for Stress Relief' and Appalachian State University's "De-Stress Fest" events, are organized during finals week to alleviate stressful exam preparations. Regular 'Meet and Greet' sessions are also standard in dormitories or libraries, thus underscoring the adaptability of therapy dog interventions to the diverse needs of older students. The impact of these programs is profound, not only in the immediate joy and relaxation they bring but also in the lasting awareness they foster about the importance of mental health.

For students in after-school programs, where the emphasis often shifts to personal development and extracurricular learning, therapy dogs play a pivotal role in building confidence, nurturing empathy, and creating inclusive communities where every student feels seen and valued.

Special Education

Within the specialized confines of unique education settings, therapy dogs assume a role that transcends the conventional, becoming integral to the educational and therapeutic strategies designed for students with autism, ADHD, and other developmental challenges. The structured predictability of a therapy dog's behavior and their capacity to engage without the complexities of human language make them ideal companions for students who find social interaction challenging. In classrooms tailored for these students, therapy dogs facilitate engagements that might otherwise be fraught with anxiety, turning them into opportunities for connection and growth. For a child on the autism spectrum, the sensory experience of petting a dog can be a calming stimulus, a bridge to sensory integration therapies that seek to navigate the world's overwhelming cacophony.

Likewise, for students with ADHD, the presence of a therapy dog can serve as a focal point, a grounding presence that aids in concentration and the management of impulsivity. The expert understanding of handlers, trained to recognize and respond to the varied needs of these students, ensures that therapy dog interventions are effective and empathetic, tailored to foster an environment where every student can thrive.

Alternative Education Programs

In alternative education programs, including juvenile detention centers and schools designed for students outside traditional settings, therapy dogs illuminate paths of rehabilitation and renewal. These environments, often marked by the presence of students who have navigated complex, sometimes traumatic life experiences, benefit immensely from the non-verbal, unconditional acceptance therapy dogs offer. Introducing a therapy dog into these settings catalyzes emotional healing, encouraging expressions of care, responsibility, and self-reflection that are pivotal to the rehabilitative process. For young individuals striving to redefine their identities and futures, the responsibility of caring for a therapy dog can instill a sense of purpose and a recognition of their capacity to nurture positive relationships. The routine and structure required in interacting with therapy dogs provide a semblance of stability, a cornerstone upon which new, healthier behavior patterns can be built. In these alternative settings, therapy dogs are not just companions but symbols of hope, embodying the possibility of change and the power of compassion to transcend even the most challenging circumstances.

Implementing Therapy Dog Teams

In conclusion, the following is a more concise bullet point list of benefits of Therapy Dogs in Schools that can be extracted for ease of communication with interested people who may not want to read this entire chapter:

1. Reduction of Stress and Anxiety

Therapy dogs have been shown to significantly reduce stress and alleviate anxiety among students. Their calming presence helps create a supportive environment conducive to learning, which is crucial for students' mental health and academic success.

2. Improvement in Mood and Overall Well-being

The presence of therapy dogs in schools has been linked to enhanced mood, self-esteem, and overall life satisfaction among students. This positive impact on students' emotional state contributes to a more positive school experience and better mental health outcomes.

3. Enhanced Social and Emotional Skills

Therapy dogs help increase student social interaction, fostering better social and emotional skills. This includes improved peer relationships and a greater sense of belonging within the school community.

4. Increased Motivation and Engagement in Learning

Therapy dogs make learning more exciting and engaging, which can lead to increased motivation and enthusiasm for school activities.

This heightened interest in learning can also reduce absenteeism and improve academic performance.

5. Improved Attendance and Academic Performance

The presence of therapy dogs has been associated with improved student attendance rates and academic performance. Creating a more inviting and supportive school environment, therapy dogs help students feel more comfortable and motivated to attend school regularly.

6. Development of Responsibility and Empathy

Interacting with therapy dogs helps instill a sense of responsibility and empathy in students. Caring for and spending time with the dogs teaches students essential life skills and fosters a sense of compassion and understanding.

7. Facilitation of Learning and Behavioral Improvements

Therapy dogs have been found to facilitate learning and contribute to gains in learning outcomes, such as reading. Additionally, their presence can improve children's behavior, making the classroom environment more conducive to learning.

8. Addressing Mental Health Crisis

The introduction of therapy dogs in classrooms is seen as a practical solution for addressing the growing mental health crisis among children and adolescents. Their presence provides emotional support and helps mitigate the effects of mental health issues.

Integrating therapy dogs in schools offers many benefits, ranging from reduced stress and anxiety to improved academic performance and social skills. These findings underscore the importance of therapy dog programs in creating a supportive and effective learning environment for students. By leveraging the therapeutic benefits of dogs, schools can enhance students' overall well-being and foster a more positive and engaging educational experience.

Chapter 6. Clarifying AAI, AAA, and AAE: Definitions for School Settings

In the specialized domain of animal-assisted programs within educational landscapes, a trio of acronyms stands at the forefront, each signifying a distinct interaction between students and animals. These are Animal-Assisted Interventions (AAI), Animal-Assisted Activities (AAA), and Animal-Assisted Education (AAE). Though subtle, the demarcation lines between these terms are crucial for educators and administrators.

Defining the terms starts with AAI, which encompasses all interventions that aim to achieve specific therapeutic goals. AAI is not merely about the presence of an animal in an educational setting but involves structured, goal-oriented activities designed to address or alleviate students' psychological, social, or physiological issues. On the other hand, AAA refers to more casual encounters with animals that, while not explicitly goal-directed, contribute positively to students' well-being and educational experience. These activities are characterized by their flexibility, spontaneity, and the absence of rigid therapeutic objectives. Lastly, AAE is the intentional inclusion of animals in educational programs to enhance learning and development. Unlike AAI and AAA, AAE is deeply integrated into the curriculum, leveraging interactions with animals to facilitate learning and reinforce educational outcomes.

Implementing Therapy Dog Teams

Contextual Use within educational settings varies broadly, reflecting different schools' diverse needs and objectives. AAI programs might be introduced to support students dealing with anxiety, providing structured sessions where therapeutic goals are pursued under the guidance of trained professionals. In contrast, AAA could manifest as regular visits by a therapy dog to classrooms or common areas, where the animal's presence uplifts moods and fosters community. AAE initiatives might integrate therapy dogs into reading programs, where reading to a dog boosts confidence and literacy skills among students.

The benefits and challenges associated with each type of interaction are multifaceted. AAI's structured approach allows for measurable improvements in student well-being, but it requires careful planning, professional oversight, and clear objectives, which can be resource intensive. AAA, while less demanding in terms of structure, relies heavily on the individual animal's temperament and the handler's expertise to navigate the less predictable nature of casual interactions. For its part, AAE offers a direct link to educational outcomes but necessitates a curriculum integration that can be challenging to design and implement. Each form of interaction, therefore, comes with its own set of considerations, from logistical to pedagogical, that schools must navigate to harness their full potential.

Implementing Therapy Dog Teams

Implementing Strategies for choosing and implementing the correct type of program hinges on a clear understanding of a school's unique context and needs; for institutions leaning towards AAI, partnerships with local therapy dog organizations can provide the necessary expertise and resources. Schools interested in AAA might focus on creating a welcoming environment for therapy dogs and their handlers, ensuring that these visits are as beneficial as possible for students and staff. For those adopting AAE, curriculum development should be collaborative, involving educators, therapists, and handlers in creating programs that seamlessly integrate therapy dogs into learning objectives.

The distinction between the Triangle and Diamond Models in AAI offers further insights into implementing these programs. The Triangle Model posits a three-point relationship involving the student, the therapy dog, and the handler, where the handler's role is primarily facilitative, allowing direct interactions between the student and the dog to drive therapeutic outcomes. Conversely, the Diamond Model introduces a professional (such as a therapist or educator) as a fourth point, creating a more complex dynamic where the professional guides the interaction towards specific therapeutic or educational goals. Each model presents its advantages and considerations, with the choice between them dependent on the objectives of the therapy dog program and the resources available within the school setting.

In navigating these definitions and models, schools are equipped to tailor animal-assisted programs that align with their educational and therapeutic objectives and respect the health of the therapy dogs at their heart. The successful integration of AAI, AAA, and AAE into school settings demands a delicate balance that honors these remarkable animals' contributions while safeguarding their health and happiness. At its core, it is a pursuit that reflects a commitment to enhancing the educational journey through the compassionate and thoughtful inclusion of therapy dogs, enriching students' lives in profound and lasting ways.

Chapter 7. More Case Studies: Real-world Success Stories of Therapy Dog Integration

The following are case studies of therapy dogs in action and the specific outcomes that proved beneficial in educational settings.

7.1 Revolutionizing Reading Programs

In a small town where literacy challenges had long cast a shadow over the youthful spirits of its school's students, a golden retriever named Benny became the unexpected hero. Benny's arrival marked the inception of a reading program unlike any the school had previously attempted. With his calm demeanor and patient presence, Benny sat beside students as they navigated the complexities of new words and sentences. Throughout the program, an astonishing transformation unfolded. Students who had once stumbled over their words began to read with newfound confidence, their voices steady and sure. Test scores bore witness to this change, with marked improvements not just in reading fluency but in comprehension as well. Teachers noted a significant shift in the students' attitudes toward reading; a task once fraught with anxiety was now approached with eagerness. Benny's influence extended beyond the pages of books; he fostered an environment where mistakes were met with encouragement, not embarrassment.

7.2 Transforming Troubled Teens

At a crossroads of adolescence, where the path often diverges towards tumultuous futures, a therapy dog named Luna offered guidance and support. Within a program designed for at-risk teens, Luna's role transcended that of a mere companion. She became a confidante, a presence that diffused the barriers teenagers had built around themselves. Through interactions with Luna, students discovered the therapeutic value of responsibility, learning to care for another being while nurturing empathy within themselves. This responsibility fostered a sense of self-worth and accountability, traits crucial for navigating the challenges of teenage years. Teachers witnessed remarkable changes in behavior — instances of aggression and defiance gave way to dialogue and cooperation. Luna's impact was a testament to the power of non-verbal communication, her ability to connect without words, and her ability to teach students the value of patience, understanding, and mutual respect.

7.3 Enhancing Emotional Well-Being in Special Education

In the specialized, unique education classroom setting, a therapy dog named Oliver became the key to unlocking students' potential. Oliver's introduction to the classroom was met with various responses, from curiosity to cautious excitement. For students grappling with the complexities of autism and ADHD,

Oliver's presence offered a unique form of solace and stimulation. His interactions with the students were gentle yet profound, encouraging non-verbal communication and promoting sensory integration through touch. Educators observed significant emotional regulation and social interaction milestones as students who previously struggled to express themselves or connect with peers began to open up. Oliver's role in the classroom exemplified the symbiotic relationship between therapy dogs and students with special needs — a bond that fosters academic progress and holistic emotional development.

7.4 Building Community and Empathy

In a school where divisions had once delineated the contours of student interactions, a therapy dog named Max became the emblem of unity and empathy. Max's presence in the school went beyond the individual benefits to students; he played a pivotal role in knitting the school community closer. Students from diverse backgrounds and social circles came together with a common purpose — to interact with, care for, and learn from Max. This shared interest cultivated inclusivity and mutual respect, breaking down the invisible barriers that had once segmented the student body. Max's influence was palpable in the hallways and classrooms, and his ability to draw students out of their shells and into the broader school community fostered a sense of belonging and togetherness. Through Max, students learned the fundamental values of empathy and compassion, lessons that resonated within the school and beyond in their homes and communities.

7.5 New Jersey Smile Program Research Data

The New Jersey Smile Program is a well-documented case study supporting the transformative potential of school therapy dog programs. The program has documented the various benefits of integrating therapy dogs into educational settings through research and data collection. The findings are compelling, revealing significant improvements in student well-being, academic performance, and social skills. The data underscores the efficacy of therapy dogs in reducing stress and anxiety among students, thereby creating an environment more conducive to learning and personal growth. Furthermore, the Smile Program has shed light on the positive impact of therapy dogs on teacher morale, highlighting the far-reaching effects of these programs beyond the student population. This research serves as a testament to the power of therapy dogs in schools and as a foundation for future initiatives aiming to harness this potential for improving educational communities.

In reflecting upon these narratives, we glimpse therapy dogs' profound influence within the educational sphere. From fostering resilience and confidence in reading programs to bridging divides within school communities, their contributions are both varied and significant. These stories, each a testament to the unique bond between humans and dogs, underscore the potential for therapy dog programs to effect meaningful change. As we transition from the tales of individual success to the broader implications for education systems, it becomes clear that integrating therapy dogs into schools is not merely an additive measure but a transformative one. The journey ahead promises to delve deeper into the mechanisms of this transformation, exploring how schools can navigate the challenges and maximize the benefits of therapy dog programs.

Chapter 8. Sculpting the Ideal Therapy Dog Team

The canvas of a school, vibrant with the strokes of daily learning and interaction, demands a therapy dog team that blends in and enhances the educational masterpiece. This chapter peels back the layers to reveal the intricacies of selecting and preparing a therapy dog for the bustling environment of a school. It's not just about picking a dog; it's about crafting a partnership that thrives in the unique education ecosystem, bringing solace, joy, and enrichment to students and staff alike.

8.1 Criteria for Choosing the Right Dog: Temperament, Health, and Breed Considerations

Temperament is Key

In selecting therapy dogs for schools, temperament stands as the cornerstone. A calm and patient demeanor, similar to the steady hand of a seasoned teacher guiding students through challenges, is non-negotiable. Recall from the initial discussions on socialization how crucial a well-balanced temperament is. Like a seasoned educator who can maintain composure and adaptability amidst classroom chaos, a therapy dog must exhibit similar resilience and flexibility. The aim is not merely to find a dog that tolerates the school environment but one that finds fulfillment and purpose within it. This requires an evaluation of the dog's reactions to varied stimuli, ensuring they remain composed and engaging when faced with the unpredictable nature of a school day.

Health Screening

Vigilance in health matters ensures the safety and well-being of both the therapy dog and the students it interacts with. This extends beyond the essential vaccinations and health checks to include regular screenings for conditions that could impair the dog's ability to function optimally in a school setting. The health of a therapy dog, much like the cleanliness of a classroom, underpins the effectiveness and safety of the educational environment. It is essential, therefore, to establish and adhere to rigorous health protocols, ensuring that the therapy dog is not only a source of emotional support but also a contributor to health and vitality within the school.

Breed Considerations

While certain breeds are renowned for their suitability as therapy dogs, it is crucial to remember that individual temperament and compatibility with the school environment are paramount. Some breeds, known for their hypoallergenic qualities, may be preferable in settings where allergies are a concern. However, the individual dog's personality, more than its breed, determines its efficacy as a therapy animal. This approach mirrors the educational philosophy that values each student's unique traits and potential, recognizing that, in the right environment, every dog, like every child, can thrive and contribute positively.

Behavioral Assessments

A comprehensive behavioral assessment serves as the litmus test for a dog's readiness to be a therapy animal in a school. This process evaluates the dog's obedience and manners and its response to unpredictable situations in a school setting. Imagine a busy school corridor during class change—students bustling about, the cacophony of voices, the sudden dropping of a book. A therapy dog must navigate this easily, maintaining its composure and readiness to engage positively with students. Thus, the assessment is not merely a hurdle but a preparatory step, ensuring the dog can handle the ebb and flow of school life with grace and patience.

Matching Dogs to School Needs

Different dog temperaments and personalities align with various school environments and objectives. For example, it considers pairing a high-energy dog with physical education programs to engage students in active play vs. matching a gentle, calm dog with reading programs that will sit patiently by as students read aloud. Thus, educators and administrators, working together, should select therapy dogs that best fit their specific educational goals and the unique atmosphere of their schools.

The introduction of therapy dog teams plays a crucial role in students' development and well-being. It enhances the educational experience, weaving compassion, understanding, and support into school life. These dogs' careful selection and preparation are not just administrative tasks but acts of dedication to creating a nurturing, inclusive, and enriching learning environment. As schools increasingly recognize the value of therapy dog programs, the criteria outlined in this section provide a solid foundation for creating compelling and truly integral teams in the school community.

8.2 The Role of Certification: Evaluating the AKC Good Citizen Training Class and Beyond

Certification stands as a testament to proficiency, signaling that a therapy dog and their handler have met established standards and are committed to maintaining a caliber of excellence essential for working within the dynamic environments of schools. The American Kennel Club's (AKC) Canine Good Citizen (CGC) program emerges as a foundational milestone in this journey, offering a structured framework through which dogs are assessed on their sociability, obedience, and adaptability—qualities paramount for a therapy dog's success in educational settings. However, this certification is the initial step leading to a deeper, more specialized engagement with the complexities of school therapy work.

Moving beyond the CGC, additional certifications and training programs carve out a trajectory for therapy dogs, equipping them with skills tailored to the unique demands of educational environments. Programs such as the Reading Education Assistance Dogs (READ) certification delve into the specifics of aiding literacy efforts by instructing dogs and their handlers on supporting children's reading journeys. Similarly, specialized training in areas such as trauma-informed approaches or sensory integration techniques equips therapy dogs to serve a broader spectrum of student needs, from those coping with stress and anxiety to students with unique learning challenges. These advanced certifications underscore a commitment to a practice that is not static but evolves in response to the changing landscapes of education and student welfare.

The certification process for a therapy dog unfolds in a series of deliberate steps, each designed to ensure that the dog-handler team is prepared for and proficient in the roles they are about to assume. Beginning with the CGC, the dog is evaluated on basic commands and behaviors indicative of good manners and social aptitude. Following this foundational certification, teams may pursue additional qualifications specific to therapy work, involving more rigorous testing scenarios that simulate the unpredictable nature of school environments. These scenarios include navigating crowded spaces, interacting with groups of children, or responding calmly to sudden noises, all aimed at gauging the dog's readiness for the complex dynamics of a school setting.

Maintaining certification is not an endpoint but a continuous journey reflective of an ongoing commitment to excellence and adaptation. Regular re-certification processes ensure that therapy dogs and their handlers remain at the forefront of best practices and are responsive to new insights and methodologies in animal-assisted interventions. This commitment to ongoing education is mirrored in the requirements set forth by certifying bodies, which often include continuing education units (CEUs) or periodic assessments to verify that the therapy dog team's skills and knowledge are current and influential.

Furthermore, this process of continuous learning and re-certification serves a dual purpose. It not only upholds the standards of the therapy dog program but also fosters an environment of perpetual growth and improvement for the dog and handler. Through workshops, seminars, and practical experiences, therapy dog teams refine their skills, expanding their capacity to contribute positively to the school community. This cycle of learning, application, and reflection ensures that therapy dog programs remain vibrant, impactful, and aligned with the evolving needs of students and educational settings.

A successful therapy dog program in schools involves rigorous certification, specialized training, and a commitment to ongoing development. Each step in the certification process, each choice to engage in further education, is a step towards fostering an environment where students can flourish. Therapy dogs, guided by the expertise and dedication of their handlers, become integral to this environment, offering comfort, encouragement, and a unique avenue for learning and growth. Through certification, therapy dog teams gain the credentials, competence, and confidence to navigate the challenges and joys of working within the vibrant world of education.

8.3 Socialization Skills for the School Environment: A Guide for Handlers

Socialization Strategies

In the complex ecosystem of a school, where the hum of learning and the rhythm of youthful exuberance converge, a therapy dog must navigate with finesse. The process of socializing these canine ambassadors to thrive in such an environment is layered, demanding a strategic approach from handlers. It begins with a deliberate introduction to the myriad stimuli they will encounter, from the echoing footsteps in hallways to the fluctuating energy levels in classrooms. Handlers play a pivotal role, gradually exposing therapy dogs to controlled simulations of school settings, incrementally increasing the complexity and intensity. This methodical exposure is comparable to weaving a net of experiences, each thread strengthening the dog's ability to adapt and respond with tranquility amidst the bustling backdrop of a school day.

Navigating Crowds and Noise

Schools are hubs of activity, with noise levels and crowd densities that can vary dramatically throughout the day. Their comfort and poise in these conditions are paramount for therapy dogs to serve effectively. Training sessions that mimic the auditory landscape of a school, from the shrillness of a bell marking the change of classes to the cacophony of a playground at recess, acclimatize dogs to these auditory stimuli. Similarly, navigating through groups of people, maneuvering calmly through a sea of legs, backpacks, and spontaneous gestures, becomes an essential skill. Handlers take on the role of guides, leading dogs through mock-ups of crowded school scenarios, rewarding calm navigation, and gradually increasing the complexity as the dog's confidence grows. This preparation ensures that the therapy dog remains composed when placed in the actual environment, undeterred by the hustle and bustle that characterizes the school atmosphere.

Interacting with Children

A therapy dog's role in a school setting is to interact with children, each with unique characteristics, abilities, and comfort levels with animals. Training for this aspect involves acclimatizing the dog to the unpredictable nature of children's movements and sounds - the sudden outbursts of laughter, the erratic running, or the clumsy, affectionate hug. Sessions that simulate these interactions, overseen by handlers who can gradually introduce the dog to a range of child-like behaviors, are invaluable. The aim is to cultivate a dog's ability to remain gentle and patient, to differentiate between playful excitement and genuine distress, and to respond with the appropriate level of engagement. This tailored approach to interaction ensures that therapy dogs can provide meaningful support to students, serving as a calming influence or an enthusiastic companion as the situation demands.

Dealing with Distractions

The school environment is rife with distractions that could divert a therapy dog's attention from their duties. The sudden drop of a tray in the cafeteria, the role of a ball across the corridor, or the scent of a lunchbox can all serve as stimuli that test a dog's focus. Training to maintain composure and obedience in the face of such distractions involves systematically introducing these elements in controlled settings. Handlers employ techniques that desensitize dogs to these common distractions, using positive reinforcement to reward focus and discipline. This process, iterative and adaptive, enables therapy dogs to distinguish between background noise and genuine cues for interaction. It ensures that the therapy dog remains attentive and engaged amidst a classroom lesson or a one-on-one session with a student, their presence an unwavering constant in the dynamic school environment.

Calibrating a therapy dog's socialization to the complex demands of school life is a progressive process. Handlers must deeply understand canine behavior and empathize with the school's rhythm and the student's needs. Through deliberate, specialized training, therapy dogs are sculpted into beings that navigate the school environment gracefully. This preparation, far from being a mere requirement, is a testament to the commitment of handlers and educators to foster an atmosphere where learning is not just about academics but about building connections, understanding emotions, and navigating the world with kindness and empathy. In the hands of skilled handlers, therapy dogs become more than just pets; they transform into integral components of the educational journey, their presence a bridge between the cognitive and the emotional, enriching students' lives in ways that reverberate beyond the classroom walls.

8.4 Custom Training Programs for Therapy Dogs: Beyond Basic Obedience

Training a therapy dog for the school setting goes far beyond basic obedience, venturing into developing programs crafted to address the diverse nature of educational environments. This section elucidates the crafting of these specialized training regimens, articulating the integration of educational objectives into therapy dog preparation, the utilization of role-playing as a pivotal training tool, and the methodologies employed in gauging the progress and efficacy of such programs.

Designing Custom Programs

Initiating the development of custom training programs necessitates a deep dive into educational settings' unique dynamics and needs. Each school harbors its culture, challenges, and triumphs, necessitating a therapy dog program that is not merely inserted but tailored appropriately within the context of each institution. This necessitates collaborations between handlers, educators, and administrators to pinpoint areas where the presence of a therapy dog could yield the most profound impact. For instance, a program to enhance emotional regulation among students might focus on training dogs to recognize and gently interrupt signs of escalating stress or anxiety. Similarly, a dog intended to assist in a literacy program would undergo training designed to encourage and engage students in reading activities by reacting positively to spoken cues or displaying attentive body language. These tailor-made programs ensure that therapy dogs are not just present within schools but are actively contributing to the educational and emotional well-being of the student body.

Incorporating Educational Goals

Incorporating educational goals into therapy dog training imbues these animals with a role that transcends their traditional therapeutic function, elevating them to partners in the academic journey. Trainers and handlers, in collaboration with educators, identify key learning objectives and integrate these into the training regimen, ensuring that interactions with the therapy dog reinforce and enhance educational outcomes. For example, a dog in a literacy program may be trained to sit attentively. At the same time, a child reads, offering physical nudges or signs of engagement at pauses, subtly encouraging the student to continue. In settings focused on social skills development, dogs might undergo training to initiate interactions that mirror typical social encounters, providing students with a safe and supportive space to practice and refine their interpersonal skills. Through this thoughtful integration of educational goals, therapy dogs become active participants in the learning process, and their presence is a catalyst for academic engagement and achievement.

Role-Playing Scenarios

The unpredictable nature of school environments, with their myriad social interactions and potential stressors, calls for a training approach that prepares therapy dogs for the wide range of situations they might encounter. Role-playing emerges as a crucial technique in this context, a method that simulates real-life scenarios within the safety of a controlled training environment. Handlers, often in collaboration with volunteers, recreate situations the dog is likely to face, from the exuberant chaos of recess to the quiet focus of a one-on-one reading session. These simulations serve multiple purposes;

they acclimate the dog to the diverse stimuli of the school setting and allow handlers to observe and fine-tune the dog's responses. Role-playing also offers a platform for practicing interventions tailored to specific behavioral or emotional challenges, ensuring that the therapy dog can easily navigate the complexities of school life. This dynamic approach to training ensures that therapy dogs are not merely present in schools but are well-prepared, adaptable beings capable of making meaningful contributions to the educational environment.

Evaluating Progress

The journey of training a therapy dog for school settings is one of continual evolution, a process that demands regular assessment and refinement. Evaluating the progress of therapy dog training programs involves a multifaceted approach, where qualitative observations and feedback from all stakeholders in the educational ecosystem are as valuable as quantitative measures. In partnership with educators, handlers establish benchmarks for success, ranging from the dog's ability to maintain calm amidst distractions to the qualitative impact of their presence on student satisfaction and engagement. Regular check-ins and structured observations of the therapy dog in action provide insights into areas of strength and opportunities for further development. Adjustments to the training program are made based on these evaluations, ensuring that the therapy dog's education is responsive to the evolving needs of the school community. This iterative process, grounded in a commitment to excellence and adaptability, ensures that therapy dogs and their handlers grow in tandem with the students and educators they serve.

8.5 Advanced Training: Addressing the Unique Needs of Diverse Student Populations

In educational enhancement through therapy dog teams, an advanced level of preparation is pivotal for addressing the needs of a student body marked by diversity. This diversity is more than merely in terms of academic or emotional requirements: it extends to the cultural backgrounds and the spectrum of sensory processing experiences that students bring into the school environment. Therefore, developing specialized training programs for therapy dogs moves beyond the foundational to embrace practices as varied and complex as the populations they aim to serve.

Customized Approaches

Creating tailored training programs for therapy dogs transcends generic methodologies, delving into the intricate landscape of specific educational and emotional needs. This entails an approach where training regimens are aligned with the distinct requirements of students, particularly those with special educational needs. For instance, a child grappling with the challenges of autism spectrum disorder might find solace in a dog trained to recognize and gently react to non-verbal cues, offering a silent but profound source of comfort. Similarly, a student battling the anxieties of a new environment, or the stresses of academic pressures benefits from a dog trained to initiate interaction with a gentle nudge or a reassuring presence, providing a tactile stimulus that soothes and grounds. These custom approaches underscore the agility and adaptability required of therapy dogs, positioning them as versatile allies in the educational journey.

Sensory Sensitivity Training

Given the kaleidoscope of sensory experiences that a school day presents, therapy dogs undergo training designed to make them attuned to the needs of students facing sensory processing challenges. This training imbues dogs with the ability to navigate these sensitivities with finesse, ensuring their interactions foster comfort rather than stress. Techniques employed include gradual exposure to various sensory stimuli under controlled conditions, and allowing the dog to become a calming presence for students who might find the sensory input of a typical school day challenging. This sensitivity extends to recognizing the cues of distress or discomfort in a student, enabling the dog to modulate its behavior in response, whether through a decrease in movement to lower sensory input or an increase in tactile engagement as a form of sensory support.

Cultural Competence

In the multicultural mosaic that characterizes contemporary classrooms, therapy dogs are prepared to engage with students from diverse cultural backgrounds, respecting how students relate to and interact with animals. This preparation involves exposure to and training in environments that mirror the cultural diversity of the student population. Handlers, too, partake in this educational journey, gaining insights into cultural norms and values that influence students' perceptions and interactions with dogs. Such competence ensures that therapy dog programs are inclusive, acknowledging and honoring the cultural identities of all students and fostering an environment where diversity is celebrated and respected.

Crisis Response

The unpredictable nature of life means schools are not immune to crises, moments when the educational community is tested. Therapy dogs, trained in crisis response, offer an example of resilience in these times, providing support that is both immediate and devoid of the complexities of verbal communication. Their preparation for such scenarios involves exposure to the chaotic environments that can accompany a crisis and training in specific behaviors that provide comfort and reassurance. For students experiencing the upheaval of emotional distress, the steady presence of a therapy dog trained to maintain calm and offer physical comfort becomes an anchor, a point of stability in the shifting sands of crisis.

The advanced training of therapy dogs, tailored to meet the student population's diverse and often complex needs, reflects a commitment to creating educational environments where every student is seen, heard, and supported. This level of preparation, marked by sensitivity to sensory needs, cultural competence, and the capacity to respond in times of crisis, positions therapy dogs not just as companions but as integral components of the educational ecosystem. They stand as a testament to the belief that education is a holistic journey, one that is enriched not only by academic achievement but by emotional growth, cultural understanding, and resilience in the face of adversity.

In synthesizing these advanced training methodologies, therapy dog programs underscore the pivotal role these animals play in fostering an educational atmosphere that is inclusive, supportive, and responsive to the different challenges and opportunities presented by a diverse student body. As we transition from the exploration of training paradigms to the practicalities of implementing therapy dog programs in schools, we carry forward the understanding that at the heart of these initiatives lies a profound commitment to enhancing the educational journey for all students. Through thoughtful preparation and dedicated training, therapy dogs emerge as vital allies in pursuing an education that celebrates diversity, nurtures emotional well-being, and cultivates a culture of empathy and understanding.

Chapter 9. Cultivating Excellence in Handlers and School Staff

A symphony without a conductor may have all the right notes, but it lacks the cohesive harmony to elevate the music. Similarly, with all their innate abilities and training, therapy dogs rely on their handlers to guide them, ensuring their interactions in schools are positive and transformative. This chapter delves into the symbiotic relationship between therapy dogs and handlers, focusing on the latter's preparation as the critical factor in successfully integrating these teams within educational settings.

9.1 Training Handlers for Success: Skills and Knowledge for the School Environment

Essential Skills for Handlers

The role of a handler extends beyond merely being at the other end of a leash. It requires a fusion of empathy, awareness, and understanding of human and canine behaviors. Handlers must possess the emotional intelligence to navigate the diverse emotional landscapes of students and the observational acuity to interpret their therapy dog's non-verbal cues accurately. This dual awareness ensures interventions are timely, appropriate, and beneficial.

Imagine a therapy dog session designed to help students with anxiety. The handler must recognize subtle shifts in the students' and dogs' demeanor, making real-time decisions to facilitate meaningful connections. This scenario underscores the handler's role as more than a supervisor; they are facilitators of interaction, a bridge connecting the therapeutic presence of the dog with the student's needs.

Behavioral Management

Understanding and managing a therapy dog's behavior in the fluctuating dynamics of a school environment is critical. Handlers receive training to preempt and address potential behavioral concerns, from overexcitement to moments of hesitation in unfamiliar settings. This involves a deep understanding of canine psychology and the ability to implement strategies that ensure the dog's behavior aligns with the goals of their school visit.

For example, if a therapy dog becomes overly excited during a lively classroom activity, the handler must employ techniques to calm the dog, maintaining the session's therapeutic atmosphere. This skill set is similar to a teacher managing a classroom, ensuring the environment remains conducive to learning and growth.

Communication Skills

Effective communication forms the backbone of any successful therapy dog program in schools. Handlers are trained to articulate the program's goals and procedures clearly to students and staff, ensuring everyone understands the purpose and potential benefits of the interaction. They also learn to listen actively, which allows them to gather feedback from the school community, adapting their approach to meet evolving needs.

An instance of this is during a pre-session briefing, where the handler explains to a group of students how to interact with the therapy dog safely and respectfully. This dialogue sets the stage for a successful session, where clear communication ensures the safety and comfort of all parties involved.

Safety Protocols

The well-being of students, staff, and the therapy dog is paramount. Handlers undergo specific training in safety protocols, learning to preemptively identify and mitigate risks associated with animal-assisted activities in schools. This comprehensive understanding of safety measures encompasses everything from managing allergies to preventing and responding to incidents should they occur.

Training handlers for success in the school environment requires a blend of empathy, behavioral management skills, practical communication, and a thorough understanding of safety protocols. This preparation ensures that therapy dog teams can navigate the complexities of educational settings, providing meaningful support to students and staff. Through this careful cultivation of handler expertise, therapy dog programs in schools not only thrive but also become integral to the educational enrichment and emotional support system.

9.2 Educating School Staff: Building Support and Understanding

Awareness Sessions

The inception of therapy dog programs within the educational sphere necessitates a foundational layer of awareness among school staff, creating a bedrock of understanding that facilitates the seamless integration of these canine companions into the daily rhythms of school life. These informational briefings and immersive experiences elucidate therapy dogs' varying roles in supporting educational and emotional health. Through presentations enriched with data, anecdotal evidence, and live interactions with therapy dogs, staff members gain firsthand insight into these animals' transformative potential. Each session is carefully crafted to address common queries and misconceptions, ensuring staff emerges informed and empowered. The goal is to broaden their perspectives about the impact of animal-assisted interventions.

Handling Interactions

The fabric of daily life in schools is textured with countless interactions. Introducing therapy dogs demands careful consideration of how these interactions unfold, necessitating clear guidelines for staff engaging with these animals. Workshops tailored to this end equip staff with knowledge of dog behavior, highlighting cues that signify contentment, anxiety, or the need for space. Practical exercises simulate real-life scenarios, offering staff hands-on experience engaging with therapy dogs, from initiating contact to reading and responding to the dog's non-verbal signals. This training ensures that every touch and word exchanged between staff and therapy dogs reinforces a positive and respectful relationship, enhancing the program's efficacy and the well-being of the dogs at its heart.

Emergency Procedures

The unpredictable nature of school environments, pulsating with the vibrant energy of youth and learning, necessitates preparedness for the unforeseen, ensuring the safety and security of students, staff, and therapy dogs alike. Training sessions dedicated to emergency procedures are helpful, instilling in staff the competencies to navigate potential incidents with composure and efficiency. These procedures cover a spectrum of scenarios, from managing allergic reactions to de-escalating situations where a therapy dog might become overwhelmed. Each staff member becomes a custodian of safety, and their actions are guided by protocols prioritizing the welfare of all participants in the therapy dog program. By embedding these procedures into the consciousness of the school community, a culture of mindfulness and vigilance is cultivated, fortifying the educational environment against the ripples of uncertainty that emergencies may bring.

Building a Supportive Environment

The alchemy of transforming schools into havens of support and understanding for therapy dog programs involves more than policy adjustments and training; it requires a shift in culture and an embracing of values that celebrate empathy, compassion, and collective well-being. Strategies to foster such an environment are diverse, involving initiatives that encourage staff to share their experiences and insights, creating a repository of knowledge that fuels continuous improvement. Recognition programs highlight and celebrate the contributions of staff who go above and beyond in supporting therapy dog interventions, their stories serving as models that inspire their peers. Through creating spaces dedicated to interaction with therapy dogs, staff will also have a tangible experience of these animals' benefits, strengthening their commitment to the program. Through these concerted efforts, a supportive environment blossoms, where therapy dogs are not merely visitors but integral school community members. Their presence is a testament to the collective commitment to nurturing students' emotional and educational growth.

In orchestrating these efforts to educate and prepare school staff for integrating therapy dog programs, a nuanced understanding of the symbiotic relationship between humans and animals unfolds. Armed with knowledge, skills, and an appreciation for the subtleties of canine behavior, staff members become active participants in this endeavor, their roles transcending the boundaries of traditional educational responsibilities. This collective journey towards embracing therapy dog programs within schools is marked by a shared vision, one where the lines between teaching and healing blur, giving rise to an educational experience that is as enriching emotionally as it is intellectually. Through the pillars of awareness, interaction, safety, and support, schools evolve into environments where learning is cradled in the compassionate presence of therapy dogs, and every hallway and classroom resonates with the silent, profound language of empathy and understanding.

9.3 Creating a Collaboration Model: Handlers, Teachers, and Administrators Working Together

The collaboration involved with school therapy dog programs, similar to an ensemble performance, necessitates a harmony of roles and responsibilities among handlers, teachers, and administrators. This concerted effort, underpinned by mutual understanding and shared objectives, fosters a conducive environment for integrating therapy dogs into the educational landscape, enhancing students' learning experience.

Developing Collaboration Strategies

The foundation of an effective collaboration strategy lies in the recognition of the unique contributions and perspectives each party brings to the therapy dog program. Drawing on the strengths of handlers, teachers, and administrators supports a cohesive framework that supports the seamless incorporation of therapy dogs into school activities. This strategy involves delineating clear objectives, aligning these with the broader educational goals of the school, and establishing a roadmap for implementation that leverages the expertise of each stakeholder. Regular interdisciplinary meetings, serving as a nexus for idea exchange and coordination, ensure that the program's direction remains aligned with the evolving needs of the school community. This collaborative process, iterative and dynamic, adapts to feedback, incorporating insights from ongoing experiences to refine and enhance the program's impact.

Role Clarification

The precise delineation of roles and responsibilities among handlers, teachers, and administrators is central to the harmonious integration of therapy dog programs in schools. This clarity ensures that each participant understands their part in the program, fostering accountability and facilitating effective collaboration. Handlers entrusted with the welfare and behavior of the therapy dogs serve as the primary link between the animals and the school community, guiding interactions to ensure they align with therapeutic and educational objectives. Teachers, as the custodians of the learning environment, integrate these interactions within their pedagogical framework, tailoring activities to enrich students' academic experiences. Administrators, overseeing the logistical and policy aspects, ensure that the program operates within the bounds of school protocols and supports the institution's broader goals. This triad of roles, distinct yet interdependent, forms the backbone of a successful therapy dog program, each contributing to its vitality and effectiveness.

Communication Channels

The fluidity of communication among handlers, teachers, and administrators acts as the circulatory system of the therapy dog program, delivering essential information and feedback that sustains and nurtures its growth. Establishing robust channels, from digital platforms facilitating real-time updates to structured debriefing sessions, ensures that all parties remain informed and engaged. These channels serve as conduits for logistical coordination and forums for sharing insights, challenges, and successes, fostering a culture of openness and continuous improvement. Through proactive and transparent communication, potential obstacles are addressed promptly, and opportunities for program enhancement are identified, ensuring its adaptive evolution in response to the dynamic landscape of the school environment.

Joint Planning Sessions

The confluence of therapy dog activities with educational goals is achieved through intentional planning. This process marries the therapeutic potential of the dogs with the curricular and extracurricular objectives of the school. Joint planning sessions, convened regularly and involving handlers, teachers, and administrators, serve as the crucible for this alignment. These sessions, characterized by collaborative brainstorming and strategic planning, explore innovative ways to integrate therapy dog interactions into classroom activities, school events, and individual student support plans. By weaving these activities into the school's educational agenda, therapy dogs become integral to the learning experience, contributing to students' emotional and social development and academic achievement. Through these collective efforts, the therapy dog program transcends its auxiliary status, becoming embedded in the school's ethos and pivotal in shaping a nurturing, inclusive, and stimulating educational environment.

In orchestrating this collaborative model, the synergy among handlers, teachers, and administrators catalyzes the successful integration of therapy dogs into schools, which enriches students' educational journey. This model, rooted in shared objectives, clear roles, effective communication, and joint planning, ensures that the therapy dog program flourishes, its impact resonant and far-reaching, touching the lives of students, staff, and the broader school community. Through this concerted effort, the promise of therapy dog programs to enhance well-being and learning through the compassionate presence of dogs is realized with the daily rhythms of school life and echoing in the corridors of education as a testament to the power of collaboration and shared purpose.

9.4 Handling Challenges: Behavioral Management of Dogs in Schools

In the dynamic school environment, therapy dogs play pivotal roles, their presence a calming balm amidst the flurry of academic pursuits. Yet, this integration is full of challenges, navigating through which requires a sophisticated understanding of canine behavior, coupled with proactive and reactive strategies that ensure the efficacy of therapy dog programs remains unblemished.

Identifying Potential Challenges

Foremost in mitigating potential behavioral challenges is the identification of scenarios that might disrupt the harmonious interaction between therapy dogs and the school populace. Predominant among these challenges are instances of overstimulation—classrooms bustling with activity can overwhelm a therapy dog's senses, leading to signs of distress or agitation. Additionally, the unpredictability of young students' actions—sudden movements or loud expressions of excitement—may elicit unexpected responses from even the most well-trained dogs. Recognizing these potential pitfalls necessitates a vigilance that is as much about understanding the environment as it is about knowing the individual dog's thresholds and triggers.

Preventative Strategies

The axiom 'prevention is better than cure' holds profound relevance in integrating therapy dogs into schools. Strategic measures aim to forestall the emergence of behavioral challenges. A cornerstone of these preventative strategies is the acclimation process, where therapy dogs are gradually introduced to the school environment, allowing them to familiarize themselves with its unique stimuli under controlled conditions. This acclimation extends to habituating dogs to the sounds and sights of school life, from the peals of laughter to the clatter of cafeteria trays, ensuring these stimuli become part of the dog's everyday experience.

Parallel to acclimation is cultivating a deep bond between the handler and the therapy dog, a relationship that becomes the dog's anchor in the sea of school activities. This bond is nurtured through consistent, positive interactions, building a foundation of trust that enables the handler to guide the dog through potentially challenging situations easily. Handlers, armed with an intimate knowledge of their canine partners, can anticipate and mitigate responses to stressors, maintaining the equilibrium necessary for the dog's successful integration into the school setting.

Intervention Techniques

Despite the most diligent preparations, challenges may arise, necessitating immediate and effective intervention to maintain the therapeutic integrity of the program. Handlers, adept in the subtleties of canine communication, employ techniques designed to recalibrate the dog's focus and alleviate stress. One such technique is the implementation of 'safe spaces' within the school, where the therapy dog can retreat to regain composure away from the bustle of school life. These spaces offer a sanctuary where dogs can enjoy quiet moments, reinforcing their sense of security.

Another pivotal intervention strategy is redirection, wherein the handler gently guides the dog's attention away from stress-inducing stimuli, refocusing it on tasks or commands that elicit calmness. Redirection defuses potential disruptions and reinforces the training and commands the therapy dog has mastered as a reminder of the familiar amidst the unfamiliar.

In instances where challenges escalate, handlers may opt for temporary removal from the environment, which allows both the dog and the students to reset. This technique is applied judiciously, ensuring the therapy dog's presence remains a positive influence within the school. Upon re-entry, the handler reassesses the situation, determining the best course of action to reintegrate the dog into activities, often utilizing gradual exposure to reduce the likelihood of recurrence. Or, it may be more appropriate to end the session and call it a day.

Learning from Challenges

Challenges are not mere obstacles but opportunities for growth and learning experiences that enrich the program and its participants. Each encountered challenge becomes a reflection node, prompting a thorough analysis of its antecedents, manifestations, and resolutions. This reflective process, embraced by handlers, educators, and administrators, fosters a culture of continuous improvement, where insights gleaned from challenges inform future strategies and training enhancements.

Handlers should document these challenges and the effectiveness of deployed interventions in concert with the school community, creating a repository of knowledge that becomes a valuable resource for the program. This documentation serves as a historical record and a guide for training revisions, highlighting areas where additional focus may yield significant benefits. Through this process, therapy dog programs evolve, their foundations strengthened by the lessons of experience, ensuring their contribution to students' educational and emotional well-being remains impactful and enduring.

Handlers and educators employ a combination of foresight, adaptability, and reflective practice in navigating the challenges inherent in integrating therapy dogs into schools. This approach ensures that therapy dogs continue to serve as examples of support within the educational landscape, their presence a testament to the resilience and collaborative spirit of those committed to enhancing students' lives through the compassionate intervention of canine companions.

9.5 Continuous Education: Keeping Skills and Knowledge Up to Date

Handlers must continue learning in the evolving landscape of therapy dog programs within schools. This pursuit is not merely a commitment to personal or professional growth but a foundational element in ensuring the vitality and efficacy of these programs. The education of handlers is a dynamic process, reflecting the ever-changing understanding of animal-assisted interventions and their application in educational settings. It involves a dedicated engagement with new methodologies, insights from emerging research, and the nuanced complexities of school environments. In this context, handlers become lifelong learners, their development paralleling the growth and transformation of the students and schools they serve.

Simultaneously, the impetus for continuous professional development extends to school staff, encompassing educators, administrators, and support personnel. This collective engagement in learning fosters an environment where the integration of therapy dogs is not just welcomed but optimized. Staff participation in workshops, seminars, and certification programs related to animal-assisted interventions enriches the school's collective knowledge base, ensuring that the presence of therapy dogs aligns with educational goals and contributes positively to the school's culture. This commitment to learning underscores the recognition of therapy dogs as adjuncts to the educational process and as integral elements that enrich the learning environment.

Staying informed about the latest developments in animal-assisted interventions demands a proactive approach. Handlers and school staff delve into academic journals, attend industry conferences, and engage with professional networks to glean new insights and strategies. This dedication to staying abreast of new knowledge ensures that therapy dog programs remain grounded in current research, enhancing their relevance and impact. The commitment to ongoing education reflects a broader understanding that animal-assisted interventions are not static but a vibrant area of study that continues to offer new insights into the human-animal bond and its applications within educational settings.

Creating forums for sharing best practices and lessons learned emerges as a critical component of continuous education. These platforms, from online forums to community meetings, facilitate a rich exchange of experiences among handlers, teachers, and administrators. They serve as incubators for innovation, spaces where challenges are dissected, strategies are honed, and successes are celebrated. This collaborative exchange amplifies the collective wisdom of those involved in therapy dog programs, fostering a culture of openness, experimentation, and mutual support. The sharing of best practices becomes a conduit for collective growth, enhancing the efficacy of therapy dog interventions and ensuring they are responsive to the needs of students and schools.

In this landscape of continuous education and shared learning, the journey of a therapy dog handler intersects with the broader mission of schools to foster environments of growth, discovery, and emotional health. This commitment to keeping skills and knowledge current, engaging in professional development, and staying informed about the latest research mirrors the journey of educators themselves. It reflects the dedication to excellence and the pursuit of strategies that enrich students' lives. The sharing of best practices and lessons learned embodies the collaborative spirit that underpins successful therapy dog programs, ensuring that these initiatives not only thrive but evolve, their impact deepening along with the educational communities they serve.

This commitment to ongoing learning, professional development, staying informed, and sharing knowledge underscores a fundamental truth: the integration of therapy dogs into schools is a dynamic process, one that thrives on innovation, collaboration, and a deep-seated commitment to students' success. As we move forward, the insights garnered from this chapter serve as a guide for the development and implementation of therapy dog programs that not only meet the needs of today's schools but anticipate the challenges and opportunities of tomorrow.

Chapter 10. Implementing Therapy Dog Teams: The Foundation

Therapy dog teams represent a pioneering approach to education, which can bring together emotional support and learning enhancement to enrich the school environment. This chapter focuses on the initial steps for effectively incorporating these teams, offering a scaffold for future animal-assisted interventions in educational institutes.

10.1 Assessing Needs and Interests

Before the paws of a therapy dog ever grace the school corridors, it's crucial to gauge the interest and necessity within the school community. A thoughtfully designed survey is a vital tool to gauge the perspectives of students, parents, teachers, and administrators. It probes the general sentiment toward having therapy dogs on campus and seeks to understand specific areas where their presence would be most beneficial. Imagine, for instance, a school where reading levels lag; here, a therapy dog program focused on literacy could ignite a passion for books among students. The survey results establish a strong groundwork, offering a clear mandate for the program's direction, backed by the collective voice of the school community.

10.2 Forming a Planning Committee

With data in hand, the next step involves assembling diverse perspectives to guide the program's inception. This planning committee, a microcosm of the school's ecosystem, brings together educators driven by innovative teaching approaches, administrators skilled in navigating the logistical labyrinths of school operations, and potential handlers who share a deep bond with their canine partners. Together, they form the core decision-making body, each member contributing their unique expertise to shape a program that aligns with the school's values and the identified needs. Their meetings, a blend of brainstorming sessions and strategic planning discussions, become the crucible in which the program's vision is refined, and its objectives are defined.

10.3 Setting Clear Objectives

Precision in goal setting is the guiding force for the therapy dog program, ensuring that each step taken moves towards a tangible impact within the school setting. Objectives, defined with specificity and measurability, cover a spectrum from enhancing student well-being to supporting specific educational outcomes. For instance, if bolstering reading skills emerges as a priority, an objective might involve increasing the number of students reading at grade level by a certain percentage within a defined timeframe. These objectives, rooted in the initial survey's insights and shaped by the committee's expertise, serve as benchmarks for the program's success, providing a clear framework against which progress can be evaluated.

10.4 Understanding the Commitment

Integrating therapy dog teams into schools is not merely a passing endeavor but a long-term commitment encompassing various aspects, including time, finances, and logistical coordination. This section illustrates the nature of this commitment, offering a candid look at the resources required to bring the vision of animal-assisted interventions to life. The logistics of scheduling visits, ensuring compliance with health and safety regulations, and coordinating with the school's calendar requires planning. This transparency serves not as a deterrent but as a foundation for realistic implementation, ensuring that the program's launch is grounded in a comprehensive understanding of the commitment required.

The foundation laid in this chapter provides a blueprint for schools navigating the initial phases of implementing therapy dog teams. From the initial assessment of community interest to the detailed planning and acknowledgment of the commitment required, each step is a building block in creating a program that not only meets the needs of the school community but also enriches the educational landscape with the unique benefits that therapy dogs offer. As schools venture into this territory, the guidance here provides the path toward a future where therapy dog teams are integral to the educational experience, enhancing the community environment and learning profoundly.

10.5 Building a Structured Program Framework: Scheduling, Sessions, and Goals

Crafting a schedule for therapy dog visits requires finesse – a delicate balance, a precise orchestration of timing that meshes with the school's existing rhythm while capitalizing on the periods when students are most receptive. This entails a deep dive into the school's daily operations, identifying slots where introducing a therapy dog would not disrupt but enhance the educational flow. For instance, scheduling sessions during less structured periods, such as after recess or before lunch, could provide students with a soothing transition, leveraging the therapy dog's presence to settle and sharpen young minds. Furthermore, aligning visits with specific classes or programs, like reading groups or stress-reduction sessions, ensures seamless integration of the dog's therapy into the curriculum's objectives.

Transitioning to session planning, the blueprint for each interaction between therapy dogs and students becomes critical. This process involves logistical considerations, such as duration and location, and a pedagogical alignment that ensures these sessions contribute meaningfully to the student's learning journey. Activities are curated with a dual focus: to foster emotional well-being and to support educational outcomes. Tailoring the length of sessions to the attention spans and needs of different age groups ensures engagement without fatigue. In addition, maintaining manageable participant numbers ensures every student can forge a personal connection with the therapy dog, making the experience both memorable and impactful.

In setting short-term and long-term goals for the therapy dog program, a vision is articulated to measure the program's success. Short-term goals might focus on immediate impacts, such as improving student mood post-session or increasing participation in targeted educational activities. Long-term ambitions, however, delve into more profound, more transformative outcomes, such as sustained improvements in reading levels or reductions in school-wide stress indicators. These goals are informed by the initial needs assessment, ensuring they are rooted in the school community's expressed desires and challenges and are revisited with regularity, allowing for adjustments as the program evolves and grows.

Cultivating a local network of therapy teams ready to visit schools marks a significant stride toward sustainability and diversity within the program. By cultivating a pool of teams readily available, schools can ensure a consistent presence, even accommodating multiple dogs to match various program objectives or student needs. Each dog's unique temperament is carefully considered, with some schools opting for a single dog that becomes a familiar figure. In contrast, others rotate dogs to provide a broader range of interactions. This strategy allows for a tailored approach to meeting educational and emotional goals and mitigates risks related to dependency on a single dog-handler team.

Flexibility and the capacity to adapt are underscored as critical virtues within the program framework. Recognizing that the needs of students, the availability of therapy dog teams, and even the program's goals are in flux, the program is designed with an inherent agility. This malleability ensures that feedback from students, educators, and handlers is heard and acted upon, allowing for the refinement of session activities, the adjustment of schedule, or even the reevaluation of goals to better serve the constantly changing landscape of the school environment. Such adaptability ensures the therapy dog program remains relevant and deeply responsive to evolving educational needs and opportunities.

10.6 Matching Dogs to Schools: Considerations for Best Fit

The intricate task of aligning therapy dog teams with the unique goals of individual schools calls for an evaluation process that transcends the mere preferences for breed or size and delves into the compatibility of temperament, training, and the handler-dog dynamic with the school's ambiance and demographic makeup. Much like a living organism, a school breathes with its rhythm, culture, and challenges. Therefore, selecting a therapy dog team that resonates with this environment is paramount.

Evaluating School Environment

The initial step in the alignment process involves a careful analysis of the school's environment. This analysis not only sketches the physical layout and size of the institution but also paints a vivid picture of its student demographics, including age ranges, cultural backgrounds, and specific educational or emotional needs. For instance, a school in a culturally diverse area might benefit immensely from a therapy dog team that exhibits exceptional adaptability and sensitivity to varied social cues and can navigate the diversity of student backgrounds with finesse. Similarly, establishments catering to students with special educational needs might discover their ideal match in a therapy dog characterized by a calm demeanor and patient presence, providing non-verbal reassurance and fostering an environment conducive to learning and exploration.

Handler-Dog Teams

The bond between a therapy dog and its handler transcends mere companionship, evolving into a partnership where both entities are finely attuned to each other and the needs of the students they aim to assist. When selecting handler-dog teams, numerous factors are considered, ranging from the handler's adeptness in navigating school environments to the dog's responsiveness to commands, even in highly distracting settings. This selection process emphasizes teams that have demonstrated a remarkable ability to collaborate harmoniously under diverse conditions, showcasing adaptability in tailoring their approaches to suit the atmospheres of different schools. The significance of this selection lies in ensuring that the handler-dog duo embodies the program's ethos, seamlessly integrating into the school's support system for its students.

Trial Visits

Trial visits act as a critical litmus test, a practical assessment that places the therapy dog team within the school's daily whirlwind of activities to observe firsthand the dynamics of interaction between the dog, the students, and the staff. These sessions, essentially rehearsals for the full integration of the therapy dog program, allow for observations on the dog's adaptability to the school's environment and the handler's efficacy in managing and directing the dog's interactions with the students. Moreover, trial visits unveil the nuances of student responses to the therapy dog's presence, offering invaluable insights into how these interactions might be optimized. For instance, a therapy dog displaying a remarkable penchant for gently engaging shy students might influence a strategic decision to focus sessions on small groups or one-on-one settings, maximizing the impact of these encounters.

Implementing Therapy Dog Teams

Feedback Mechanisms

Establishing robust feedback mechanisms is integral to refining the match between therapy dog teams and schools. These systems, designed to capture a spectrum of perspectives from the school community, serve as a conduit for insights, suggestions, and evaluations of the therapy dog program's impact. Feedback, harvested through digital surveys, focus group discussions, and informal conversations, becomes the cornerstone for iterative improvements, ensuring the therapy dog's presence resonates positively within the school. This back-and-forth loop of feedback and adjustment ensures that the therapy dog program remains responsive and deeply integrated into the school's culture, evolving in tandem with the shifting landscapes of educational and emotional needs.

The process of matching therapy dog teams to schools, marked by an evaluation of school environments, careful selection of handler-dog teams, insightful trial visits, and dynamic feedback mechanisms, embodies a commitment to excellence and sensitivity in meeting the needs of school communities. Through this process, therapy dog programs are tailored to become not just an intervention but a transformative presence within schools, offering support, comfort, and enrichment that are finely tuned to the unique rhythms and needs of each educational setting.

10.7 Engaging Parents and the Community: Gaining Support and Building Awareness

The success of a therapy dog program in educational environments isn't confined to the walls of the school alone. Its influence extends beyond the community and students' homes, where parents and local entities hold pivotal roles. The essence of this extension lies in cultivating a deep understanding and strong support network that surpasses the immediate educational realm, embedding the program into the broader consciousness of the community.

Information Sessions

The journey of expansive engagement commences with crafted information sessions aimed at disseminating knowledge and captivating the interest of parents and community members. These gatherings, infused with the warmth of communal interaction, serve as platforms where the profound impact of therapy dogs on children's well-being and academic progress is vividly depicted. Through compelling storytelling and the presentation of empirical data, these sessions shed light on the many benefits of therapy dog programs, ranging from nurturing a supportive school environment to catalyzing enhancements in student engagement and learning outcomes. Incorporating testimonials from other schools, embellished with anecdotes of transformation and growth, adds credibility and breathes life into the potential of these programs. Thus, these sessions transcend mere dissemination of information, acting as conduits for fostering a collective vision for the holistic benefit of the student body.

Communication Materials

Parallel to the direct engagement of information sessions, the strategic deployment of communication materials plays a crucial role in sustaining the dialogue with the school community and the wider public. Newsletters, elegantly designed and rich with stories of moments shared between students and therapy dogs, offer a regular glimpse into the program's ongoing impact. Flyers, brief yet powerful in their message, serve as reminders of the program's presence and its open invitations for community involvement. Social media posts, vibrant and engaging, harness the power of digital platforms to reach beyond the immediate geographic confines, inspiring a broader audience and fostering a digital community of supporters. In their varied formats, these materials ensure that the narrative of the therapy dog program remains a persistent whisper in the ears of the community, inviting ongoing engagement and support and encouraging greater volunteer participation.

Involving Students and Parents

The heart of the program's integration into the school and its community beats strongest when students and parents become advocates and participants. Encouraging the formation of clubs centered around the therapy dog program provides students with leadership opportunities. It also offers a platform to contribute to the program's shaping directly. Projects that allow students to explore and present on the science of human-animal bonds or the history of therapy dogs in educational settings deepen their understanding and cultivate a sense of ownership and pride in the program. Including therapy dog-related activities within the curriculum, through reading projects or science lessons on animal behavior, further solidifies this engagement. Welcoming parents as volunteers for the program, whether in the capacity of coordinators for therapy dog visits or as contributors to program materials, fosters a deeper connection and investment in the program's success. This collective involvement of students and parents enriches the program with diverse perspectives and cements its place within the school's culture as a valued and vital component.

Community Partnerships

Opportunities to establish partnerships with local businesses, nonprofits, and media outlets are highly encouraged. These alliances are forged to enhance the well-being and educational experience of the community's youth. Recognizing the value of supporting educational initiatives, local businesses may offer sponsorships or host fundraising events, providing financial or in-kind support that sustains and expands the program. Nonprofits focused on animal welfare or youth services become natural allies, offering resources, expertise, and networks that enrich the program's offerings. Media partnerships with local newspapers, radio stations, or TV channels amplify the program's reach, drawing in support and interest from corners of the community previously untouched. Through these collaborative endeavors, the therapy dog program gains valuable resources. It secures a prominent place in the heart of the community narrative, recognized as a tool for innovation in education and student support.

This comprehensive approach to engaging parents and the community, from information sessions and communication materials to direct involvement and partnerships, provides a robust support network around the therapy dog program. It ensures that the program is seen not as an isolated endeavor but as a communal asset, valued and upheld by many stakeholders. Through this collective embrace, the program finds footing and the momentum to thrive and expand, touching more lives and shaping a future where therapy dogs are an integral part of the educational landscape, supported and celebrated by all.

10.8 Documentation and Record-Keeping: Tracking Progress and Impact

In the dynamic landscape of educational settings, where

therapy dog programs are interwoven into daily school life, documentation and record-keeping emerge as pivotal elements. When established with precision and care, these processes function as the backbone for assessing the subtle impacts of these interactions on the school's atmosphere, the students' learning experiences, and their emotional lives. Setting up efficient systems for this purpose transcends mere administrative tasks, evolving into a strategic framework that captures the essence of each session, including who was present, the nature of the activities conducted, and the immediate feedback provided by participants.

Measuring the program's impact is a complex endeavor that relies heavily on surveys and observations. These findings can be designed to capture data reflecting shifts in student engagement, well-being, and academic performance. Employed with analytical precision, these tools provide expansive and detailed insights, offering a sophisticated understanding of how interactions with therapy dogs resonate throughout the student body and the educational environment. For example, surveys administered to students before and after therapy dog sessions could unveil shifts in self-reported stress levels, offering tangible evidence of the program's efficacy in enhancing emotional tranquility. Concurrently, observations by educators during these sessions might reveal subtle but significant changes in student behavior, such as increased participation or improved focus, metrics that speak volumes about the program's impact on the learning climate.

Regular reporting of progress to stakeholders is a testament to the program's commitment to transparency and continuous improvement. These reports, crafted with clarity and depth, convey the successes and milestones achieved, the challenges encountered, and the lessons gleaned from them. This practice of sharing insights extends beyond the confines of the program's immediate circle, reaching out to parents, community members, and educational authorities, ensuring all vested parties are apprised of the strides. This act of reporting fosters a culture of accountability and mutual support, which provides feedback that can help shape future directions for dog therapy programs.

At the heart of these endeavors lies the principle of data-driven decisions. This philosophy champions empirical evidence as the foundation for making informed choices regarding program adjustments and expansions. This steadfast commitment to an evidence-based approach ensures that every step and modification is rooted in a clear understanding of the program's dynamics and its tangible impacts on the school setting. Whether it involves expanding the program to include additional therapy dogs, adjusting session formats to better suit student needs, or introducing new activities based on observed interests, decisions are guided by the r data collected through diligent documentation and insightful analysis as well as by comparisons with other schools in varying districts and states.

The twin pillars of documentation and record-keeping serve as guiding lights. They illuminate the path forward, ensuring that each stride is informed by a deep understanding of the program's effects on the educational landscape. The gathering of data, thoughtful analysis of impact, and transparent sharing of progress lay the groundwork for a program that is effective, adaptable, and responsive to the evolving needs of students and the broader school community.

This commitment to rigorous documentation and insightful analysis paves the way for a future where therapy dog programs are recognized for their immediate charm and profound and lasting impacts on educational environments. It sets the stage for a deeper exploration of the strategies and methodologies for successful integration, ensuring these programs continue to grow, evolve, and enrich students' lives in meaningful ways.

Chapter 11. Nurturing Safe Bonds: Health and Safety in Therapy Dog Programs

In education, the paramount significance of health and safety cannot be emphasized enough. This chapter delves into the strategies and protocols that form the bedrock of a secure, nurturing environment for students, staff, and therapy dogs. It's comparable to preparing a garden for spring; just as gardeners enrich the soil, remove hazards, and prioritize the health of their plants, schools must cultivate a safe space for therapy dog interactions to flourish.

11.1 Allergy Management Plans

In the same way that a curated menu caters to the dietary restrictions of all guests at a banquet, schools must develop and implement comprehensive plans to manage and minimize the impact of allergies among students and staff. This involves detailed mapping of potential allergens and strategies such as designated dog-free zones and thorough cleaning protocols following therapy dog visits. In addition, clear communication channels must be established. It allows those with allergies to voice their concerns and receive assurance of their safety. Additionally, proactive measures, such as hypoallergenic breed selections, dog types that do not shed, and regular grooming of therapy dogs, further mitigate allergy risks, ensuring the inclusivity of the program. Schools with therapy dogs must send forms home to identify students and staff with known allergies or aversions to dogs, which would alert handlers to avoid those uncomfortable for these reasons.

11.2 Safety Protocols

Therapy dog interactions require a set of well-defined safety protocols that guide every step of the process. These protocols encompass guidelines for handling and behavior, ensuring that dogs remain calm and controlled, even in the bustling environment of a school. Regular training sessions for both dogs and handlers reinforces these guidelines. Hygiene practices, such as using hand sanitizers before and after contact with the dog, become as routine as washing hands before a meal, ingrained in the daily habits of students and staff.

11.3 Incident Response

In every well-oiled machine, there are contingencies for the unexpected; therapy dog programs are no exception. Creating clear procedures for responding to and documenting incidents or injuries involving the therapy dog is similar to having a first-aid kit and emergency plan in a home. These procedures outline immediate steps for addressing the situation, from administering first aid to notifying relevant authorities and parents. A designated incident logbook is a comprehensive record, detailing events to improve future preventive strategies. This level of preparedness instills confidence within the school community, reassuring them that safety remains a top priority.

11.4 Regular Health Checks

The health of therapy dogs is the cornerstone upon which the program's safety rests. Regular health screenings, performed by qualified veterinarians, ensure that dogs are free from diseases that could be transmitted to humans. These check-ups include vaccinations, parasite control, and general wellness exams, mirroring the preventive healthcare recommended for children. Schools might consider maintaining a health passport for each therapy dog, a document that logs vaccinations, screenings, and any medical interventions, providing a transparent record of the dog's health status. This proactive approach to health care ensures that therapy dogs are happy, healthy, and safe student companions.

In orchestrating therapy dog programs, the harmony of health and safety protocols with the daily rhythms of school life is non-negotiable. It requires vigilance, commitment, and a deep-seated respect for the well-being of all participants. Through the implementation of allergy management plans, the establishment of safety protocols, the readiness of incident response procedures, and the assurance of regular health checks for therapy dogs, schools lay down the foundation for a program that enriches the educational experience without compromising safety. This chapter, a testament to the care and planning for these programs, offers a blueprint for schools to navigate the complexities of integrating therapy dogs into their communities, ensuring that every child can safely experience the joy and comfort these furry companions bring.

11.5 Navigating Cultural Sensitivities and Individual Fears

The landscape of an educational environment is a vibrant collage, rich with the hues and textures of diverse cultural backgrounds and personal experiences. Within this setting, introducing therapy dog programs necessitates a delicate, attuned approach to cultural sensitivities and individual apprehensions surrounding animals. This sensitivity is not merely an adjunct to the program but a vital component, ensuring its acceptance, effectiveness, and the comfort of all participants.

11.6 Cultural Awareness Training

Diverse attitudes towards animals, shaped by cultural norms and religious beliefs, necessitate an informed, respectful approach to introducing therapy dog teams to schools. To this end, cultural awareness training for handlers and staff emerges as a critical measure, equipping them with the knowledge and skills to navigate these varied perspectives gracefully and understanding. This training explores global cultural attitudes towards dogs, delving into the historical, religious, and social underpinnings that inform these views. By cultivating an environment of respect and empathy, the program fosters a space where cultural differences are acknowledged and celebrated, ensuring that therapy dog interactions enrich experiences that bridge cultural divides rather than exacerbate them.

Individualized Approaches

Recognizing the individuality of each student's experience with and reaction to animals is paramount. For some, the presence of a therapy dog in the school may evoke discomfort or fear stemming from past experiences or phobias. In these instances, the program's flexibility is its strength, offering alternative activities that ensure no student is alienated or feels compelled to participate against their comfort. These alternatives are not afterthoughts but are designed with the same intentionality as the primary program. They ensure that students who opt out still receive support and engagement opportunities that contribute to their situations and sense of inclusion in the school community. This personalized approach underscores the program's commitment to meeting each student where they are, honoring their feelings, and providing paths to participation that respect their boundaries.

Open Dialogue

At the core of a therapy dog program lies a foundation of understanding and mutual respect anchored by the pillars of open dialogue. This dialogue takes the form of proactive conversations with students, parents, and staff, creating a forum where concerns can be voiced, questions can be asked, and information can be shared freely. These conversations are opportunities to demystify the therapy dog program, addressing misconceptions and clarifying its goals, benefits, and safety protocols. The program fosters a sense of ownership and participation by inviting input from all corners of the school community. It ensures that cultural sensitivities and individual apprehensions are addressed with empathy and action. This ongoing dialogue creates a feedback loop that enriches the program, making it a dynamic, evolving entity that reflects the community it serves.

Inclusive Practices

The hallmark of a genuinely inclusive therapy dog program lies in its practices. These practices should reflect a deep commitment to creating an environment of accepting and embracing diversity. Inclusivity is the guiding principle, from selecting therapy dogs and their handlers to designing activities and the spaces where interactions occur. For instance, the program might include therapy dogs of various sizes and breeds, reflecting the diversity of the school's student body and providing points of connection for students from different cultural backgrounds. Activities are designed to be universally engaging, transcending language barriers and cultural differences and promoting shared experiences that foster community and mutual understanding. The physical spaces where therapy dog interactions occur are chosen and arranged to be welcoming and accessible to all students, ensuring that no physical or cultural barriers impede participation.

School therapy dog programs embark on a delicate journey as they navigate the myriads of cultural sensitivities and individual fears. This journey, guided by cultural awareness training, individualized approaches, open dialogue, and inclusive practices, is one of respect, understanding, and empathy. It acknowledges the diverse backgrounds and experiences of the student body, ensuring that the therapy dog program is a source of comfort, engagement, and enrichment for all. Through these concerted efforts, the program not only achieves its goals of supporting students and enhancing the educational experience but also becomes a magnet for inclusivity, reflecting the values of respect and understanding at the heart of the educational mission.

Chapter 12. Funding and Budgeting for Your Program: Creative Strategies and Resources

Securing the financial foundation for a school therapy dog program demands a creative approach and strategic insight. It is like assembling a quilt, where each piece, whether it's a grant opportunity or a community fundraiser, contributes to creating a supportive and sustainable financial structure for the program. This endeavor extends beyond mere monetary concerns, embedding itself in the community engagement and partnership ethos that therapy dog programs espouse. Districts in states including Virginia, Oklahoma, Michigan, and Colorado have used portions of the $123 billion in K-12 relief funding provided by the American Rescue Plan to fund specialized therapy dog training.

12.1 Grant Opportunities

Seeking grant funding is not merely a matter of submitting applications; it involves a sophisticated exploration of alignment between the program's objectives and the mission of potential grantors. This alignment is crucial to ensure that the funding provided supports the program's logistical needs and advances its impact on the educational ecosystem. Navigating this terrain requires a deep understanding of the diverse grant opportunities available, ranging from those focused on educational innovation to others dedicated to animal-assisted interventions. Each application presents a compelling narrative that encapsulates the program's vision, its demonstrated or potential impact on student well-being, and its alignment with the grantor's objectives. This process is iterative, with each submission refined through feedback and evolving insights, ensuring that the pursuit of grant funding remains strategic and adaptable. Since the program's inception in 2010, Pets in the Classroom has awarded over 218,215 grants to teachers, meaning an estimated 8.7 million children have experienced the joys and benefits of pet care through the grant program. As teachers look for more ways to help with students' social-emotional needs, the Pets in the Classroom grant program is ready to help by providing funding for classroom pets to pre-K – 9th-grade teachers across the U.S. and Canada.

12.2 Community Fundraising

Community fundraising events are more than just avenues for financial support; they are vibrant expressions of the program's place within the heart of the community. These events serve multiple purposes, from charity runs with therapy dogs to school fairs where the dogs are the stars. They raise funds, build awareness, foster community spirit, and demonstrate the program's value. The planning and execution of these events hinge on creativity and community engagement, ensuring that each fundraiser resonates with the local culture and interests. Partnerships with local businesses for sponsorships or in-kind donations add depth to these events, embedding them further into the community's social life. The success of these fundraisers lies not just in the funds raised but in the strengthened bonds between the program and the community it serves.

12.3 Partnerships and Sponsorships

Cultivating partnerships and sponsorships with local businesses and philanthropic organizations represents a strategic approach to securing support that transcends financial contributions. These relationships are built on shared values and a mutual commitment to enhancing the educational landscape. From pet stores to bookshops, local businesses may offer sponsorships or donations of goods and services, enriching the program's resources and providing students with enhanced experiences. Philanthropic organizations dedicated to education or animal welfare can become allies, offering funding, expertise, and networks that amplify the program's reach and impact. Stewarding these relationships is critical, involving regular updates and demonstrations of the program's outcomes, ensuring that partners are closely connected to the program's successes and challenges. This stewardship fosters a sense of joint investment in the program's goals, making each partner an integral part of the program.

<u>Other potential funding sources:</u>

1 FUR 1 Foundation: The 1 FUR 1 Foundation offers therapy grants for programs that require membership of volunteer teams by nationally recognized certification programs such as Pet Partners, Therapy Dogs International, Alliance Therapy Dogs, and PATH International. They also provide grants for service/assistance dog programs, but applicants must be accredited members of Assistance Dogs International.

DonorsChoose: DonorsChoose is a trusted classroom funding site for teachers. Teachers can create projects to request funding for specific needs, such as a licensed therapy dog to provide physical and emotional health benefits to students.

Charlotte's Litter Therapy Dog Program advocates for therapy dog programs in educational settings and is committed to providing financial support to K-12 schools that provide these services. The Charlotte's Litter Grant Program accepts grant applications all year and determines eligibility twice a year, in January and August. Charlotte's Litter is a program of the Charlotte Helen Bacon Foundation.

12.4 Budget Management

Effective budget management acts as the keystone in the arch of program sustainability. It involves the tracking of expenses and income and the strategic allocation of resources to maximize impact. This transparent and efficient management ensures that every stakeholder understands the program's financial condition. The system used for this tracking is accessible, allowing for real-time updates and facilitating strategic decisions regarding program activities and expansions. This transparency builds trust, ensuring donors, partners, and the school community feel confident supporting the program. Also, this approach helps identify financial challenges before they become crises, enabling proactive adjustments to ensure the program's continued viability.

Initiating therapy dog programs with volunteer teams presents an invaluable strategy for schools navigating financial constraints. This approach leverages the goodwill and commitment of local dog owners willing to share their pets' therapeutic benefits without immediate compensation. It provides a low-cost entry point for schools to pilot the program, demonstrating its value and building a case for further investment. While modest in scale, these volunteer-led initiatives can catalyze broader community support and serve as a foundation for the program's expansion. The success of these volunteer-driven efforts hinges on clear communication, robust support from the school, and recognition of the volunteers' contributions, ensuring that these foundational teams feel valued and connected to the program's overarching goals.

Navigating the financial landscape of therapy dog programs in educational settings demands creativity, strategic planning, and a deep commitment to community engagement. From the pursuit of grant opportunities and the vibrant energy of community fundraising events to the cultivation of meaningful partnerships and the diligent management of finances, each strategy contributes to the program's sustainability. More importantly, the strategic use of volunteer teams offers a pathway for programs to establish their value, laying the groundwork for future growth. This comprehensive strategy for funding ensures that therapy dog programs can continue to enrich students' lives, fostering environments where learning and emotional well-being flourish hand in hand.

Chapter 13. Evaluating and Adapting the Program: Feedback Loops and Continuous Improvement

The importance of designing a structured process for evaluation stands out as an instrumental tool for the benefit of all therapy dog programs. This process, similar to systematically observing a carefully tended garden, allows for assessing growth and vitality and identifying areas requiring nurturance or change. Continuous evaluation transcends mere oversight, embodying a commitment to excellence and the unwavering pursuit of enriching the school environment. The program undergoes a rigorous examination at designated intervals, leveraging both quantitative metrics and qualitative insights to gauge its effectiveness. This evaluation considers a spectrum of factors, from the observable impact on student engagement and well-being to the subtler shifts in the school's social dynamics attributed to the presence of therapy dogs. Instruments of measurement are diverse, encompassing surveys that capture the voices of the school community, analyses of academic performance data, and observational studies that offer snapshots of interactions between students and therapy dogs.

Feedback, the lifeblood of the program's evolution, flows from myriad sources, each providing a unique lens through which the program's impact is viewed. Students articulate their experiences, shedding light on how therapy dog visits influence their emotional landscape and academic journey. Staff and educators reflect on the program's integration into the school's daily routines and alignment with educational goals. Parents, observing the ripples of the program's influence on their children's attitudes towards school, contribute their perspectives, enriching the program's validity. Handlers, too, share insights drawn from their intimate understanding of the therapy dogs' reactions and adaptability to the school environment. This feedback, collected with intentionality and respect for each contributor's viewpoint, becomes a cornerstone for the program's reflective practices.

The program can respond to this feedback with agility, adjusting its structures, activities, and goals. Adaptation is not seen as an admission of shortfall but as a natural step in the program's lifecycle, similar to the seasonal shifts in a garden that dictate changes in care and cultivation. These adjustments may manifest in various forms, from introducing new activities designed to deepen the therapy dogs' engagement with students to modifications in scheduling that align more closely with the school's rhythms. Changes are informed by a blend of feedback, research findings that offer new insights into animal-assisted interventions, and the evolving needs of the school community. This adaptation process is iterative, with each alteration as a stepping stone in the program's journey toward deeper integration and more significant impact.

Innovation, the spark that drives the program towards uncharted territories, is encouraged and nurtured. New ideas, whether stemming from advances in educational theory, breakthroughs in animal-assisted therapy research, or creative suggestions from the school community, are explored with an open mind. These innovations may include novel approaches to integrating therapy dogs into specific curriculum areas, leveraging technology to enhance the program's reach, or developing partnerships that expand the program's resources and scope. Each innovative practice undergoes thorough evaluation to assess its potential to improve the program, with successful initiatives seamlessly integrated into its operations. This spirit of innovation ensures that the therapy dog program remains at the forefront of educational enrichment strategies, continually evolving to meet the needs of a dynamic educational landscape.

The cyclical evaluation, feedback, adaptation, and innovation process forms a robust framework for continuously improving the therapy dog program. This framework, reflective of a commitment to excellence and responsiveness, ensures that the program not only meets the current needs of the school community but anticipates and adapts to future challenges and opportunities. Through this process, the therapy dog program solidifies its role as a vital component of the educational ecosystem, contributing to a nurturing, supportive, and enriching school environment for all.

Chapter 14. Building Resilience: Ensuring Program Sustainability

Within the fabric of a school, where the threads of education and emotional support intertwine with students' lives, therapy dog programs add a layer of comfort and companionship, enhancing the complex challenges of learning. However, the longevity and effectiveness of such initiatives hinge not just on their immediate success but on their ability to endure and adapt over time. This endurance is cultivated through strategic foresight, community engagement, various supporting documentation, and a commitment to the continual growth of those at the program's heart.

14.1 Long-Term Planning

The horizon of a therapy dog program stretches far beyond the present, requiring a vision that anticipates future needs, challenges, and opportunities. This vision is encapsulated in a long-term plan that serves as a roadmap, guiding the program's evolution. Crucial to this planning is the consideration of handler and dog succession, ensuring that the departure of critical individuals does not leave a void but rather an opportunity for renewal. Schools must foster relationships with training organizations and therapy dog associations to maintain a pipeline of qualified handlers and dogs. Additionally, this planning encompasses the program's expansion, setting measurable goals for increasing its reach and depth within the educational community. Through this forward-looking lens, the program secures its place and adapts to the changing landscape of academic needs and therapeutic practices.

14.2 Community Support

The roots of a therapy dog program's resilience lie in the soil of community support, nourished by the engagement and commitment of students, parents, educators, and local partners. This support is not merely a backdrop for the program's operations but a dynamic force that propels it forward. Schools must cultivate this support through regular communication, sharing the successes and stories from the program, and inviting community participation in its planning and execution. Events showcasing therapy dogs and their positive impact on students serve as bridges, connecting the school with the broader community and fostering a shared investment in the program's success. Once ignited, this communal spirit becomes a sustaining flame, ensuring that the therapy dog program remains a cherished and vibrant aspect of the educational landscape.

14.3 Documentation and Legacy

The history of a therapy dog program, with its milestones and moments of transformation, is a treasure trove of insights and inspiration. Maintaining thorough documentation of the program's activities, achievements, and challenges creates a rich legacy that informs future iterations of the program and serves as a model for other schools embarking on similar journeys. This documentation includes detailed records of sessions, feedback from participants, and assessments of the program's impact on student emotional health and academic performance. Beyond serving as a practical resource, this legacy is a narrative of progress, chronicling the journey of a community united by the therapeutic presence of dogs in their midst. By sharing this narrative through publications, presentations, and digital platforms, the program extends its influence, inspiring others and contributing to the broader dialogue on animal-assisted interventions in education.

14.4 Professional Development

The vitality of a therapy dog program is mirrored in the growth and development of its handlers and associated staff. Investing in ongoing professional development ensures that these individuals remain at the forefront of best practices in animal-assisted therapy, educational strategies, and safety protocols. Workshops, seminars, and certifications offer avenues for learning and advancement, equipping handlers and educators with the tools and knowledge to enhance the program's effectiveness. This commitment to professional growth fosters a culture of excellence and innovation within the program, ensuring that it not only meets the current needs of the school community but also evolves to embrace new methodologies and insights.

As the chapter on ensuring program sustainability ends, reflecting on the pillars underpinning a therapy dog program's endurance reveals strategic planning, community engagement, consistent documentation, and professional growth. These elements create a resilient structure that supports the program's longevity and effectiveness. The journey forward for therapy dog programs in schools is continuous adaptation and renewal, guided by a vision that embraces change and values the profound impact of human-animal bonds on the educational experience. With eyes set on the future, these programs stand as testaments to the power of compassion, companionship, and community in enriching students' lives. The next chapter will explore the process of integrating therapy dogs into the curriculum, solidifying their role in fostering a supportive and dynamic educational environment.

Chapter 15. Legal Frameworks and Ethical Considerations

In the realm of educational innovation, the introduction of therapy dog programs adds a complex pattern of legal and ethical intricacies. Just as schools must adeptly navigate evolving guidelines in public health, they must also carefully address these vital aspects, which are essential for the integrity of the programs. This chapter examines these legal and ethical dimensions, similar to the precision of a surgeon's hand, thereby enabling schools to effectively integrate therapy dog programs while adhering to legal and ethical standards.

15.1 Understanding Federal and State Legal Guidelines for Therapy Dogs in Schools

Navigating Laws

The legal framework surrounding therapy dogs in educational environments is comprised of a patchwork of federal and state statutes. Each piece contributes to a comprehensive understanding of the responsibilities and rights governing these programs. Federally, laws like the Americans with Disabilities Act (ADA) and the Individuals with Disabilities Education Act (IDEA) establish broad guidelines, notably distinguishing between service animals and therapy dogs—an essential differentiation for schools to grasp. However, state-level regulations introduce further complexities that can vary significantly across jurisdictions, covering everything from handler qualifications to animal welfare standards.

Navigating this legal complexity demands careful attention, much like a librarian organizing a vast collection of literature, ensuring each book finds its rightful place on the shelf. For instance, while the ADA clearly outlines the rights of service animals, therapy dogs are afforded different protections under this legislation. Understanding these distinctions is crucial to avoid unintentional legal pitfalls.

15.2 Compliance Strategies

Compliance in this context is less about adherence to a static set of rules and more about an ongoing engagement with the legal landscape. It involves regular reviews of state and federal law changes, much like how a gardener must stay attuned to shifts in weather patterns, adjusting care strategies to ensure plants thrive. Schools might establish a legal review committee comprising legal experts, administrators, and therapy dog handlers, which functions much like a weather station, forecasting legal changes and preparing the program to adapt.

15.3 Recent Changes

Legal shifts have mirrored broader societal changes in recent years, reflecting increased recognition of therapy dogs' value. For example, some states have expanded access rights for therapy dogs, recognizing their role in supporting mental health and learning. Keeping abreast of these changes is similar to tracking technological advancements; just as educators integrate new tech tools to enhance learning, so must we incorporate recent legal shifts into the operational aspects of therapy dog programs.

15.4 Case Law Insights

Examining case law offers a prism through which schools can view potential legal challenges and solutions. These cases serve as navigational guides, illuminating schools' paths. For instance, a case where a school faced litigation for denying access to a student's therapy dog underscores the need for clear policies and procedures. Reviewing such cases, schools can anticipate challenges and fortify their programs against similar legal pitfalls.

15.5 Legal Checklist for Therapy Dog Programs

A visually organized and easy-to-navigate detailed checklist can give schools a tangible tool to review their compliance with legal standards. This checklist covers critical areas such as handler certification, dog health and welfare, student and staff rights, and program documentation. Much like a pilot's pre-flight checklist ensures every detail is noticed, this legal checklist offers schools a systematic approach to ensuring their therapy dog program is legally compliant and ethically sound.

15.6 The Ethics of Animal-Assisted Interventions: Best Practices Ethical Considerations

In integrating therapy dogs within school settings, a lattice of ethical considerations forms the framework for scrutinizing and validating these programs. Central to this ethical inquiry is the recognition of therapy dogs not merely as tools for educational and therapeutic ends but as sentient beings with needs, rights, and well-being that must be safeguarded and respected. This perspective necessitates thoroughly examining the moral obligations owed to these animals, ensuring their school deployment does not compromise their welfare. This ethical lens extends to the students and staff interacting with these therapy dogs, ensuring their engagement is marked by respect, understanding, and consent. The moral matrix within which therapy dog programs operate demands vigilance to navigate its dimensions successfully.

15.7 Ensuring Animal Welfare

The imperative to ensure the welfare of therapy dogs in schools mandates a proactive, informed approach that prioritizes these animals' physical and emotional health. Best practices include health checks, regular veterinary care, and keen attention to the signs of stress or discomfort exhibited by therapy dogs during their student interactions. The environments in which these dogs work must be assessed for safety, providing spaces that allow for rest and retreat, ensuring they can withdraw from interactions should they feel overwhelmed. Furthermore, the scheduling of therapy dog visits must reflect understanding the animal's capacity for work, avoiding overexertion, and ensuring adequate rest periods between sessions. This commitment to animal welfare underscores the ethical foundations of therapy dog programs. It enhances the quality of interactions between dogs and students, fostering genuine, positive exchanges rooted in mutual satisfaction.

15.8 Informed Consent

The principle of informed consent plays a pivotal role in ethically managing therapy dog programs, prioritizing students' and their families' autonomy and rights. This involves sharing information about the program's nature, potential benefits, risks, safety measures, and well-being assurances. Parents and guardians receive detailed information, empowering them to make informed decisions regarding their child's involvement. Similarly, students have a voice in the process, allowing them to express their comfort levels or concerns about interacting with therapy dogs. This inclusive approach ensures that participation is based on genuine willingness and enthusiasm, fostering an environment of trust and respect that enriches the therapeutic and educational aspects of the program.

15.9 Balancing Needs

The ethical integrity of therapy dog programs is further evidenced by balancing the needs and rights of students, staff, and therapy dogs. This balance requires a deep understanding of the diverse dynamics at play within the school setting, recognizing that the welfare of one party should not be advanced at the expense of another. For instance, strategies are developed to accommodate students with allergies or phobias, ensuring their educational experience remains uninterrupted and upbeat while allowing their peers to benefit from the therapy dog program. Similarly, therapy dog handlers' rights and responsibilities are delineated, ensuring they are equipped and supported in their role while also being held to standards that safeguard the welfare of the dogs in their care. This equilibrium is maintained through ongoing dialogue, feedback, and adjustments, reflecting a commitment to an ethical program that honors and responds to the varied needs within the school community.

The ethical landscape of animal-assisted interventions in schools is characterized by its depth and complexity, demanding a vigilant, informed approach to navigate its contours successfully. At the heart of this ethical endeavor is a profound respect for the dignity and respect of therapy dogs and a commitment to ensuring their integration into educational settings enhances, rather than diminishes, their quality of life. This respect extends to the students and staff interacting with these animals, ensuring their experiences are marked by consent, understanding, and mutual benefit. Schools can foster therapy dog programs that exemplify ethical integrity and compassionate education by diligently applying best practices in animal welfare, informed consent, and balancing needs.

Chapter 16. Developing a School Policy for Therapy Dog Integration

Crafting an all-encompassing policy that is the backbone for integrating therapy dog programs within the educational setting requires planning, similar to an architect designing a building with beauty and functionality in mind. While layered and complex, this process ensures that the program adheres to legal and ethical standards and aligns with the school's educational objectives and community values.

16.1 Creating a Comprehensive Policy

The initial phase in sculpting such a policy is similar to laying the foundation of a house, where every brick must be placed with precision and foresight. Schools must first assemble a task force, a blend of educators, administrators, legal advisors, therapy dog handlers, and, where possible, representatives from the student body and their guardians. This team begins drafting the policy, articulating the program's scope, objectives, and operational guidelines. The drafting process is iterative, requiring rounds of discussion, revision, and refinement. Key areas of focus include defining the roles and responsibilities of handlers, specifying the criteria for therapy dog selection, outlining the procedures for student participation, and establishing protocols for monitoring and assessing the program's impact. Each clause and provision is crafted to safeguard the welfare of the therapy dogs and the students they serve while enhancing the educational environment.

16.2 Key Components

The policy's effectiveness and sustainability hinge on several foundational elements. Firstly, it's crucial to clearly outline the program's objectives, whether it's enhancing student literacy, fostering social development, or offering emotional support. Next, specific guidelines for selecting and training therapy dogs and their handlers ensure that only teams meeting rigorous standards participate. In addition, the policy must establish procedures for obtaining informed consent from students and their families, prioritizing individual autonomy and transparency. Another vital aspect is implementing a structured framework to evaluate the program's outcomes, facilitating ongoing refinement and alignment with the changing needs of the school community.

16.3 Stakeholder Involvement

The involvement of stakeholders in the policy development process is not merely a procedural step but a foundational principle that ensures the policy reflects the diverse perspectives and needs within the school community. This inclusive approach fosters a sense of ownership and commitment among all participants, from the educators and staff who implement the program to the students and families who will experience its benefits. Stakeholder engagement is facilitated through forums, surveys, and discussion groups, avenues that express hopes, concerns, and suggestions. The insights garnered from these engagements are invaluable, imbuing the policy with a depth and richness that could not be achieved otherwise. While demanding in terms of time and effort, this collaborative process cultivates a policy that is robust, comprehensive, and deeply resonant with the community it serves.

16.4 Policy Review and Adaptation

The final stage in the policy's life cycle is characterized by an ongoing commitment to review and adaptation. Recognizing that both the educational landscape and insights into animal-assisted interventions are continually evolving, the policy must be a living document, adaptable to discoveries, changing legal requirements, and the shifting dynamics of the school environment. Periodic reviews are scheduled, drawing on data collected from program evaluations, feedback from stakeholders, and developments in the field of therapy dog research. These reviews are opportunities for reflection and recalibration, ensuring that the policy remains aligned with its foundational goals while also responsive to new opportunities for growth and improvement. Adjustments made through this process are communicated to all stakeholders, ensuring that the policy serves as a clear and practical guide for the program's operation.

Schools undertake a challenging and gratifying task in crafting a policy for therapy dog integration. Through a process marked by planning, inclusive stakeholder involvement, and a commitment to continuous improvement, schools lay the groundwork for programs that enrich the educational experience and foster well-being among students. This carefully sculpted and regularly refined policy is a testament to the school's dedication to creating a supportive, dynamic, and compassionate learning environment.

Chapter 17. Risk Management and Liability: Creating a Safe Environment

17.1 Assessing Risks

The foundation of integrating therapy dog programs within the academic environment is predicated on an analysis of potential hazards, a process analogous to charting a map through unexplored territories where every detail, from the elevation of the land to the density of the forest, informs the path forward. This risk assessment, conducted with the precision of an auditor examining the books of a multinational corporation, involves a systematic review of the school's physical environment, the characteristics of the student population, and the specific attributes of the therapy dog teams. Identifiers such as areas with high foot traffic, spaces prone to noise levels that might agitate dogs, and the diverse needs of students, including those with allergies or fears of dogs, are cataloged. The process unfolds through a series of observations, consultations with experts, and reviews of incident reports from similar programs, culminating in a document that not only outlines potential risks but also ranks them according to their likelihood and potential impact, providing a clear vision of where preventive measures are most critically needed.

17.2 Mitigation Strategies

Upon identifying and prioritizing risks, developing strategies to mitigate these potential hazards is similar to a chess master planning several moves, anticipating the opponent's strategy, and positioning pieces to safeguard the king. Mitigation strategies in this context involve incorporating physical adjustments to the school environment, such as creating designated therapy dog areas that are both welcoming and contained, and procedural changes, like establishing guidelines for student behavior around dogs. Training for the therapy dogs and their handlers is intensified, focusing on scenarios identified as higher risk, ensuring they are equipped to navigate the complexities of a school setting with aplomb. Additionally, communication protocols are established, ensuring swift action and clear reporting lines in the event of an incident. This measure serves as both a deterrent and a response mechanism.

17.3 Insurance Considerations

The exploration of insurance options to cover therapy dog programs is undertaken with the thoroughness of a navigator plotting a course through stormy seas, where every current and wind pattern is examined to ensure safe passage. Schools explore a range of insurance products, seeking policies that offer comprehensive coverage for incidents involving therapy dogs, including potential injuries to students or staff and any harm that might come to the therapy dogs themselves. This search for insurance is conducted in consultation with legal advisors and insurance professionals, ensuring the chosen policies meet the school's needs and comply with state and federal regulations. The selection of insurance coverage is a critical step, providing a financial safety net that enables the school to proceed with the therapy dog program confidently, knowing that both the unexpected and the foreseeable are accounted for.

Some professional organizations, such as the Alliance Of Therapy Dogs, provide certified members with insurance that covers volunteer therapy dog visits as long as all the rules are followed in their handbook. Some homeowners' policies will also cover therapy dog interactions. Also, school handler's homeowners' insurance or supplemental policies are available.

17.4 Incident Response Plans

The crafting of incident response plans is approached with the attention to detail of a composer arranging a symphony, where each note and rest is carefully placed to achieve a harmonious outcome. These plans are predicated on scenarios identified during the risk assessment phase, outlining specific actions to respond to various incidents, from minor injuries to more significant emergencies. Developing these plans involves input from a wide range of stakeholders, including therapy dog handlers, school administrators, healthcare professionals, and legal advisors, ensuring a comprehensive and practical approach to incident management. Training sessions are held for all involved parties, simulating potential incidents to ensure the response becomes second nature, reducing the potential for panic and ensuring a coordinated, effective reaction. The existence of these detailed incident response plans serves as a testament to the school's commitment to the safety and well-being of its students, staff, and the therapy dogs that walk its halls, providing a structured framework for action that underscores the program's foundation in careful planning and proactive management.

Chapter 18. Privacy and Confidentiality in Therapy Dog Sessions

Navigating privacy and confidentiality within therapy dog sessions in schools requires a delicate balance that upholds the sanctity of personal experiences while nurturing trust and security. This task involves recognizing the vulnerability inherent in these interactions, where students often share their emotions and thoughts in the presence of a therapy dog. While therapeutic, this scenario necessitates stringent safeguards to protect their privacy rights.

Understanding these privacy rights involves recognizing the dual role of therapy dog sessions as spaces for emotional release and educational support. It becomes imperative to delineate the boundaries of what information is shared, with whom, and under what circumstances. This understanding is rooted in the legal frameworks that govern student privacy, such as the Family Educational Rights and Privacy Act (FERPA) in the United States, which sets the stage for developing protocols that ensure students' personal information and the details of their interactions with therapy dogs remain confidential.

Best practices for preserving confidentiality during these sessions stem from a commitment to establishing a secure environment where students feel free to express themselves without apprehension of judgment or exposure. This necessitates clear guidelines for handling and documenting session notes, restricting access to authorized personnel, and implementing a secure storage system to prevent unauthorized entry. Developing consent forms that clearly outline how session information may be utilized, shared, or stored further reinforces this protective barrier, ensuring that students and their guardians comprehend the privacy measures.

The ethical and legal considerations of recording and sharing information from therapy dog sessions add another layer of complexity to the privacy equation. While capturing moments from these sessions, whether through notes, photographs, or videos, can provide valuable insights for program evaluation and improvement, it also raises questions about consent and the potential for unintended privacy breaches. Here, the ethical imperative to not harm guides the decision-making process, necessitating explicit consent from all involved parties and a clear purpose for the recording that aligns with the program's educational and therapeutic objectives. This careful consideration ensures that the integrity of the therapy dog sessions is preserved, safeguarding the privacy and dignity of the students involved.

Navigating sensitive situations that may arise during therapy dog interactions calls for an adaptive strategy that recognizes the fluidity of emotions and the potential for disclosures that require confidentiality. Handlers and school staff are trained to manage these situations with discretion, ensuring that any disclosures made in the context of a therapy dog session are addressed following established privacy protocols and, when necessary, referred to appropriate support services within the school. This adaptive approach is underpinned by ongoing training that equips all involved with the skills to maintain confidentiality, manage sensitive information, and respond to students' needs with empathy and professionalism.

In conclusion, safeguarding privacy and confidentiality within therapy dog sessions transcends mere procedural necessity; it is a cornerstone of the trust and security underlying these vital interactions. Through an approach that upholds students' privacy rights, adheres to best practices for confidentiality, and navigates the intricacies of recording and sharing session information, schools establish a solid foundation for therapy dog programs that honor the emotional vulnerability of students while fostering a safe, supportive environment for growth and healing. This steadfast commitment to privacy and confidentiality ensures that therapy dog sessions continue to be a cherished part of the school experience, where students can seek solace, companionship, and support without compromising their right to privacy.

As we look towards the future and explore further avenues to enrich and expand the impact of animal-assisted interventions in education, the lessons learned in safeguarding privacy and confidentiality serve as guiding principles, ensuring that the well-being of students remains at the forefront of our efforts.

Chapter 19. Evaluating the Echoes of Paws in Halls: Crafting Metrics for Therapy Dog Programs

In the ever-evolving landscape of educational enrichment, the gentle patter of paws echoing through school corridors heralds a symphony of potential transformations. The presence of therapy dogs within these revered halls not only alters the immediate atmosphere but also promises to weave a deeper narrative of emotional and academic growth. This chapter delves into the systematic crafting of metrics, a task similar to a cartographer charting the uncharted territories of the impact these canine companions create within the educational sphere.

Aligning success metrics with a therapy dog program's objective transcends mere procedural formality; it serves as the cornerstone of understanding and amplifying its impact. Like seasoned gardeners who understand that the true measure of their labor extends beyond the visible bloom to the fertility of the soil beneath, educators and administrators must look beyond surface-level indicators to assess the profound changes these programs catalyze.

19.1 Developing Success Metrics: What to Measure and Why

Defining Objectives

Objectives for therapy dog programs often transcend

traditional academic goals, touching upon emotional support, social skill enhancement, and fostering a nurturing school environment. Articulating these objectives requires a clarity that mirrors the precision of a skilled craftsman, ensuring that each goal is measurable and deeply rooted in the program's purpose. For instance, while one program might reduce student anxiety, as evidenced by decreased visits to the school counselor, another might focus on enhancing reading skills and tracking improvements through literacy testing scores.

Varied Metrics for Holistic Evaluation

The introduction of varied metrics acknowledges the profound impact of therapy dog programs, spanning emotional health, academic performance, and staff satisfaction. This variety necessitates a toolkit approach, employing different tools to measure distinct impact areas. Just as a doctor uses a stethoscope to listen to the heart and a thermometer to gauge body temperature, educators might use student self-report scales to assess emotional health and standardized test scores to measure academic impacts.

Setting Benchmarks

Establishing benchmarks serves as a navigational aid, offering points of reference that signal progress or indicate areas needing adjustment. These benchmarks, rooted in the objectives of the therapy dog program, provide a clear vision of success against which real-time data can be measured. In practical terms, if a program aims to improve reading scores, a benchmark might be set at a 10% improvement within the academic year, offering a tangible goal that galvanizes effort and focus.

Customization for Context

Customizing metrics to fit each school's unique context underscores the recognition that no two educational environments are the same. This tailoring process respects each school's culture, needs, and objectives, ensuring the metrics measure impact and resonate with the community's values and goals. For example, in a school where absenteeism is a pressing concern, metrics might prioritize tracking attendance rate changes after introducing a therapy dog program.

Educators undertake the gratifying task of developing success metrics for therapy dog programs. By defining clear objectives, embracing a variety of metrics, setting tangible benchmarks, and customizing these measures to suit the unique landscapes of their schools, they establish a framework for comprehending the profound and enduring impact of these programs. Integrating an interactive dashboard into this process brings the data to life, offering insight into the emotional and academic transformations unfolding within the school walls graced by therapy dogs. Through this process, the gentle echoes of paws in the halls are translated into a language of growth, change, and enrichment, charting a course for the future of educational enrichment through animal-assisted interventions.

19.2 The Role of Surveys and Questionnaires: Gathering Feedback from Teachers and Students

In educational innovation, where empathy, knowledge, and care are intertwined with the noble aim of fostering a nurturing atmosphere, the crafting of surveys and questionnaires emerges as a pivotal instrument. This tool, designed with attention to detail, serves as a conduit, channeling participants' myriad experiences, perceptions, and insights through the prism of structured inquiry. The essence of this endeavor lies not merely in the act of questioning but in the art of listening—transforming the raw, often unarticulated feedback from teachers and students into a coherent narrative that guides the continuous evolution of therapy dog programs.

Designing Effective Tools

Creating these feedback instruments transcends the simple enumeration of queries; it demands an acute sensitivity to the subtleties of human experience and a profound understanding of the program's objectives. Questions are sculpted with the precision of a master jeweler, ensuring that each serves as a key, unlocking the depths of participants' perceptions, experiences, and emotions. This process involves a deliberate layering of questions, from those that solicit direct responses regarding the tangible aspects of the therapy dog program to more open-ended inquiries that invite reflection on the subtler, transformative impacts of these canine companions. The design also incorporates measurement scales, allowing for a gradation of responses that captures the spectrum of participant engagement and impact.

Frequency and Timing

The rhythm of administering these surveys and questionnaires is orchestrated to harmonize with the academic calendar, ensuring that the timing maximizes participation while minimizing disruption. The selection of these moments is strategic, aiming to capture feedback when the experience with therapy dogs is fresh in the participants' minds and when the program has had sufficient time to manifest its impacts. This balance is similar to the timing of a photographer, who, in pursuit of the perfect photograph, must patiently wait for the moment when light, subject, and composition align. Within this temporal framework, the surveys are disseminated, and their frequency is calibrated to provide snapshots at intervals that allow for the accumulation of experiences, ensuring a rich, detailed accumulation of feedback.

Analyzing Feedback

Analyzing the feedback gathered is an exercise in intellectual alchemy, transforming the raw data of personal experiences into golden insights that inform the program's path forward. This process involves layering analytical techniques, from the straightforward tallying of quantitative responses to the more thematic analysis of qualitative feedback. Patterns emerge from this analytical crucible, revealing not only the direct impacts of the program but also the subtler, more significant shifts in the school environment—shifts in attitudes, the emotional climate of classrooms, and the connections between students and the broader school community. This analysis is reflective and forward-looking, identifying areas of success to be celebrated and areas for refinement or reimagining.

Actionable Insights

The culmination of this process—the distillation of feedback into actionable insights—mirrors the work of a cartographer, who translates the undulating landscapes of the earth into a map that guides travelers on their journeys. These insights function as signposts, illuminating the program's strengths and spotlighting the pathways toward enhancement. Actionable insights may reveal, for instance, the need for more frequent therapy dog visits to specific classrooms, adjustments in the program to better serve students with particular needs, or opportunities to expand the scope of activities within which therapy dogs are involved. Each insight catalyzes discussion among educators, administrators, and handlers, fostering a collaborative approach to program adaptation that is responsive, dynamic, and deeply attuned to the needs and experiences of the school community.

In this pursuit, the role of surveys and questionnaires transcends mere assessment tools, embodying a profound commitment to listening, understanding, and acting upon the feedback of those who live the daily reality of the therapy dog program. Through this continuous inquiry, analysis, and action cycle, the program evolves and deepens its roots within the educational community, becoming an integral thread in the school's culture. This process, marked by thoughtful design, strategic timing, careful analysis, and a commitment to actionable insights, ensures that the therapy dog program remains a vibrant, impactful presence in the lives of students, a testament to the power of empathy, care, and collaboration in the noble pursuit of educational enrichment.

19.3 Observational Studies: Seeing the Impact in Action

Therapy dogs' interactions with students have refined effects, subtle yet profound in their depth and breadth. Capturing these moments requires an approach that goes beyond traditional data collection methods. Structured observation stands as a sentinel, vigilant in documenting the silent dialogues and unspoken transformations facilitated by these gentle creatures. This method, similar to an artist capturing a fleeting moment on canvas, demands observers to immerse themselves in the environment. Their senses must be attuned to the dynamics of each interaction, free from preconceptions or biases.

The training of these observers is an endeavor marked by rigor and a dedication to objectivity. Each observer embarks on a journey of learning that equips them with the skills to navigate the delicate balance between involvement and detachment. This training encompasses an understanding of canine behavior and communication, enabling observers to discern the subtleties of dog-student interactions, from the gentle nudge of a dog seeking attention to the quiet retreat of a student finding solace in the dog's presence. With this viewpoint, observers are instilled with an awareness of their biases, recognizing the lens through which they view the world and how it might color their observations. Through exercises in reflective practice, they learn to set aside these biases, approaching each observation with a fresh perspective, unburdened by expectations or judgments.

Balancing the collection of quantitative and qualitative data within this framework presents a challenge similar to navigating a ship through waters where currents of objective measurement and subjective experience converge. With its precision and comparability, quantitative data offers a scaffold upon which the program's impact can be quantified. It provides markers of attendance rates, academic performance improvements, and behavioral changes. Yet, it is the qualitative data, with its depth and richness, that breathes life into the numbers, offering insights into the emotional journey of students as they interact with therapy dogs. Narratives of breakthrough moments, descriptions of shifts in classroom dynamics, and reflections on the personal growth experienced by students and staff alike are gathered, each a thread in the broader story of the program's impact. This dual approach ensures a comprehensive view, capturing the measurable outcomes and the intangible changes that permeate the school environment.

Addressing the ethical considerations inherent in observing students within this context is undertaken with the gravity and care of a custodian safeguarding a precious treasure. At the heart of this ethical landscape is respecting the privacy and dignity of all participants, guiding every aspect of the observational process. Consent is sought from the guardians of the students and the students themselves, ensuring they understand the nature of the observation and its purpose. Observers are trained to maintain a discreet presence, their observations are non-intrusive, and their interactions with students and therapy dogs are respectful and mindful of boundaries. Confidentiality is paramount, with measures in place to ensure that all data collected is anonymized, safeguarding the identity of participants and preserving the sanctity of their experiences. This rigorously upheld ethical framework ensures that the observational studies yield valuable insights and do so in a manner that honors the school community's trust in the program.

In this process of structured observation, the impact of therapy dog interactions within the educational setting is illuminated, revealing a landscape where emotional growth, learning, and connection flourish. Observers, trained to navigate this landscape with objectivity and sensitivity, link the silent testimonies of these interactions and the broader narrative of the program's impact. Through their eyes, therapy dog programs' subtle yet profound effects are brought to light, contributing to a deeper understanding of their value in fostering an environment where students thrive. This endeavor, marked by a commitment to rigor, objectivity, and ethical integrity, ensures that the silent echoes of paws in halls are heard, understood, and recognized for their educational enrichment and emotional support.

19.4 Data Analysis: Interpreting Results for Program Improvement Tools and Techniques

In data interpretation, the analytical process unfolds, mirroring an artisan crafting a masterpiece from raw materials. The information gleaned from therapy dog sessions, designed from surveys, observational studies, and performance metrics, transforms various analytical tools and techniques. At the outset, descriptive statistics offer a foundational understanding, painting a broad strokes picture of the data's landscape. This is like sketching the initial outline of a painting, where frequencies, means, and modes lay the groundwork for deeper inquiry.

Progressing to more complicated tools, inferential analysis unearths the latent narratives within the data, drawing connections and conclusions that extend beyond the immediacy of the collected information. Techniques such as regression analysis, t-tests, and ANOVA (Analysis of Variance) illuminate the relationships between variables, uncovering the subtle influences of therapy dog interactions on student outcomes. This analysis phase is similar to adding layers of color and texture to a painting, where each brushstroke enriches the overall composition, revealing intricacies previously obscured.

Identifying Patterns and Trends

Determining patterns and trends within the data requires an astute observational eye reminiscent of a naturalist discerning the signs of changing seasons within the subtle cues of the environment. Patterns emerge as consistent threads, weaving through the data, signaling areas of significant impact or unexpected outcomes of the therapy dog program. For instance, a recurring increase in student engagement metrics following therapy dog visits would highlight a consistent benefit analogous to flowers' reliable bloom with spring's advent.

Conversely, trends indicate directional shifts over time, offering insights into the evolving nature of the program's impact.

These might manifest as gradual improvements in academic performance or shifts in the social dynamics of the classroom, similar to the slow but observable growth of a tree, marking the passage of time with its expanding canopy. Identifying these patterns and trends necessitates a blend of analytical precision and intuitive insight, allowing program administrators to navigate the data with the confidence of a seasoned sailor reading the stars.

Reporting Findings

Conveying these findings to stakeholders is an art form that requires distilling complex analyses into accessible, compelling narratives. This process is facilitated by visuals—charts, graphs, and infographics—that serve as windows into the data, offering clear, immediate insights at a glance. These visuals act as bridges, translating the abstract language of statistics into a form that resonates with the diverse audience of educators, parents, and community members.

The narrative accompanying these visuals is crafted with a keen awareness of its audience, employing clear, non-technical language that invites understanding rather than obfuscation. The data is then added to a story that highlights key findings, acknowledges limitations, and suggests areas for further inquiry. It is a delicate balance like a poet choosing just the right words to evoke a scene, capturing the essence of the program's impact in an informative and inspiring manner.

Continuous Improvement Cycle

At the heart of this analytical journey is the principle of continuous improvement. This cycle propels the therapy dog program towards ever-greater levels of efficacy and enrichment. The insights fueling this cycle are garnered from data analysis, and each evaluation cycle feeds into the next program development phase. It is a process marked by iteration and adaptation, responsive to the shifting landscapes of educational needs and the evolving understanding of animal-assisted interventions.

Integrating data analysis into this cycle ensures that decisions are grounded in evidence, providing a solid foundation for building program enhancements. Adjustments may range from refining therapy dog selection criteria to introducing new session activities to address identified needs. This reflective and dynamic process ensures that the therapy dog program remains a vibrant, evolving entity within the school, attuned to its students' needs and the community's aspirations.

Chapter 20. Case Study Compilation: Sharing Success Stories for Broader Impact

The narratives of change—those stories that emerge from the quiet intersections of student lives and canine companions—are invaluable treasures. These stories, rich with the hues of personal growth and communal harmony, serve not merely as testaments to the program's success but as evidence that lights the path for others. The selection of these narratives, careful crafting of their telling, and the strategic dissemination to a broader audience form a triad of steps that amplify the impact of therapy dog programs far beyond their immediate circles.

20.1 Selecting Impactful Stories

In curating case studies, the selection criteria pivot on the depth of impact and the breadth of experience encapsulated within each narrative. The goal is to spotlight a range of outcomes, from the subtle shifts in a child's confidence to the sweeping changes in a school's culture, thereby ensuring the comprehensive representation of diverse benefits. This selection process mirrors the discernment of a curator in an art gallery, where each exhibited piece is chosen for its capacity to evoke emotion, stimulate reflection, and catalyze action. These narratives undergo thorough scrutiny against a set of criteria, ensuring that each selected story not only bears testament to the transformative potential of therapy dog programs but also resonates with a broad audience, serving as a mirror in which they can discern their own aspirations.

20.2 Storytelling Techniques

When applied to these case studies, storytelling involves a delicate balancing act—merging factual accuracy with emotional resonance. The stories are structured to draw the reader into the experience, employing vivid descriptions, relatable emotions, and clear articulations of outcomes. The narrative arc of each case study guides the reader from the initial context, through the challenges faced, to the resolutions and revelations brought about by the intervention of therapy dogs. This narrative journey is punctuated with direct participant quotes, offering authentic voices that lend credibility and depth. The aim is to craft stories that inform and move the reader, stirring a sense of possibility and a desire to bring about similar transformations within their contexts.

20.3 Dissemination Strategies

The channels through which these stories are disseminated are as diverse as the audiences they intend to reach, spanning from digital platforms like blogs and social media to traditional media outlets and academic journals. Each platform is carefully selected based on its capacity to engage a particular segment of the broader community, ranging from educators and policymakers to parents and prospective program volunteers. Furthermore, presentations at educational conferences and workshops provide live forums for sharing these case studies, facilitating direct interaction with the audience and fostering discussions. This multi-channel dissemination strategy guarantees that the impact stories resonate far and wide, planting seeds of inspiration across diverse landscapes.

20.4 Inspiring Change

The ultimate aim of sharing these success stories is to ignite a spark of change, motivating other schools and communities to consider integrating therapy dog programs into their educational ecosystems. These stories serve as both proof of concept and a roadmap, showcasing the tangible benefits while offering valuable insights into the implementation process. Much like the ripple effect caused by a pebble dropped into a pond, this inspiration extends beyond the immediate readership, sparking conversations, fostering advocacy, and ultimately leading to the adoption of therapy dog programs in new contexts. These narratives of transformation become catalysts, propelling a movement that advocates for the holistic well-being of students and the innovative enrichment of educational environments.

The integration of therapy dog programs represents a convergence of empathy, science, and community; storytelling emerges as a vital force. These narratives of transformation— thoughtfully selected, imbued with emotional and educational depth, and shared across various platforms—serve as evidence of the program's success and as sources of inspiration. They invite reflection, stimulate dialogue, and inspire action, contributing to a broader movement that recognizes the value of incorporating the compassionate presence of therapy dogs into educational settings. By weaving together, the threads of these narratives, this chapter highlights the profound impact of therapy dog programs and casts a vision for their potential to enrich educational landscapes. As we transition from celebrating successes to exploring future horizons, the stories shared here serve as a solid foundation for further innovation and exploration, promising new chapters of growth and discovery in the ongoing journey of educational enrichment.

Chapter 21. Expanding Horizons: Enriching the Canine Tapestry in Schools

Their presence creates a rich emotional and academic uplift tableau as therapy dogs tread the school corridors. Against this backdrop, the momentum of success sparks contemplation about growth and the subtle expansion of this harmonious blend of compassion and education. Scaling the program, however, requires the precision of a skilled gardener who understands that a flourishing garden depends on careful planning. It's about nurturing the soil, understanding the ecosystem, and anticipating the needs that new seeds will bring to the garden's existing harmony.

21.1 Identifying Opportunities for Growth: When and How to Expand

Initial steps resemble a gardener assessing the health and spread of their plants; it's an in-depth evaluation of the therapy dog program's current reach and impact. This assessment is rooted in tangible outcomes—measured improvements in student well-being, quantifiable advancements in learning, and palpable shifts in the school's social systems. Tools for this assessment vary, from surveys capturing the school community's pulse to data analytics painting a broader picture of the program's effects. This analysis lays the groundwork, pinpointing where the program thrives and where it harbors the potential for further growth.

21.2 Identifying Needs and Opportunities

Identifying growth avenues is similar to a horticulturist pinpointing the spots in a garden where new plants could add more color and diversity. It involves an analytical examination of the school's and community's evolving needs, discerning gaps the program could fill. For instance, a nearby school might express interest, or there may be a need for more specialized sessions to cater to different student groups. This stage focuses on aligning the program's expansion with genuine needs, ensuring that growth is organic and meaningful.

21.3 Strategic Planning for Expansion

Creating a strategic expansion plan is akin to architecting a complex addition to a well-loved building. This plan includes detailed objectives, timelines, and the resources required to achieve the envisioned growth. It's a blueprint that considers the logistical aspects of scaling—training more dogs and handlers, extending the program to new sites, and integrating advanced technologies or methodologies. This plan doesn't just aim for expansion; it strategizes sustainable growth that preserves the program's essence while extending its reach.

21.4 Sustainability Considerations

Ensuring the long-term sustainability of the expansion effort is like a gardener ensuring their garden not only blooms this season but continues to thrive for years to come. It involves a critical assessment of resources—both human and financial—and a keen eye on the program's ability to maintain its quality and impact as it grows. Questions of handler burnout, financial strains, and the potential dilution of the program's effectiveness come to the fore. Solutions might involve seeking partnerships, exploring new funding avenues, or implementing volunteer-driven models to support the expanded program's needs.

In therapy dog programs within schools, expansion is not merely about extending boundaries but also enriching the support these canine companions provide. It's a thoughtful process that balances ambition with mindfulness, ensuring that as the program's reach widens, its roots remain firmly planted in the principles of compassion, education, and mutual growth. Through planning, strategic execution, and a steadfast commitment to sustainability, the program sets the stage for a future where more students, schools, and communities can experience the profound impact of these remarkable animals.

21.5 Training More Dogs and Handlers: Scaling Your Resources

Recruitment Strategies

In the quest to enhance therapy dog programs, the initial step lies in augmenting the cadre of dogs and their human counterparts. Far from a mere accumulation of numbers, this endeavor mirrors the cultivation of a garden where each new plant is selected for its potential to thrive and enrich the ecosystem. The strategies to attract more dogs and handlers require a thoughtful approach that appeals to the community's sense of service and the deep, often untapped, desire to make a difference. Local partnerships with dog training clubs, veterinary associations, and animal shelters serve as fertile grounds for recruitment, each offering a unique pool of potential candidates whose skills and attributes may align with the program's needs. Social media campaigns and community outreach events cast a wider net, drawing in those whose lives have been touched by therapy dogs or who are interested in contributing to educational enrichment. The message is disseminated through these channels as a call for participation and an invitation to join a movement that bridges human and canine capabilities for mutual growth.

21.6 Standardized Training Programs

The need for a standardized training regimen becomes clear as new teams are brought under the program's expanding umbrella. This framework ensures that each dog and handler duo has the foundational skills required for their roles and is aligned with the program's core values and methodologies. Creating such a curriculum is like drafting a map for a journey through uncharted territories, where each skill learned acts as a compass point guiding the way. Core modules cover a spectrum of essential topics, from canine behavior and communication to navigating educational environments, ensuring that every team is prepared for the challenges and rewards of their roles.

Additionally, this training emphasizes the importance of adaptability and continuous learning, preparing handlers to meet the evolving needs of the students and schools they serve. Standardizing the training ensures consistency in the quality and impact of the program across all its dimensions, laying a solid foundation upon which the expansion can securely rest.

21.7 Mentorship Programs

Within the heart of the program's growth lies the mentorship component, a crucial mechanism that facilitates the seamless integration of new handlers and their canine partners. This initiative pairs seasoned program veterans with newcomers, creating a bridge that transfers knowledge, experience, and insights through one-on-one interactions and shared experiences. Much like the apprenticeship of a craftsman, the mentorship journey is characterized by observation, practice, and feedback, allowing novices to refine their skills under the watchful eyes of their more experienced peers. This process is enriched by the diversity of experiences and perspectives within the mentor pool, offering differing views of the program's possibilities and challenges. Through this intimate collaboration, new handlers gain technical competencies and an ingrained sense of the program's ethos, ensuring they carry forward its legacy of compassion and efficacy.

21.8 Ongoing Support and Professional Development

The program's development continuously supports growth opportunities, recognizing that the journey of a therapy dog team is one of perpetual evolution. Ongoing support mechanisms, including advanced training workshops, peer support groups, and resource access, ensure that handlers and their canine partners always move towards greater mastery of their roles. These resources offer guidance and assistance through the challenges and questions that arise during their duties.

Additionally, professional development opportunities, ranging from conferences and seminars to online courses, keep handlers at the forefront of knowledge in animal-assisted therapy. This commitment to ongoing growth enhances the capabilities of each team and elevates the program, ensuring it remains a dynamic, impactful force within the educational landscape.

By orchestrating these strategies, the program enhances a richer fabric of support and enrichment for the schools it serves. It expands its reach through careful recruitment, rigorous training, thoughtful mentorship, and a commitment to continuous professional development. All of this strengthens the entire program, deepening its impact and ensuring lasting benefits for the educational community.

Chapter 22. Collaborating with Other Schools: Building a Network

In the vast and variegated landscape of educational innovation, the operation and expansion of therapy dog programs stand as a testament to the enduring power of collaboration. The process of intertwining a network of partnerships among schools is marked by its potential to amplify the benefits of these programs, transcending the boundaries of individual institutions to foster a broader community of support, learning, and mutual enrichment.

22.1 Identifying Potential School Partners

The initial foray into this collaborative venture requires a discerning eye for potential partners. These schools not only exhibit a readiness to embrace the therapy dog initiative but also possess the capacity to contribute to the collective wisdom of the network. Criteria that guide this selection process span the logistical feasibility, ideological alignment, and the complementarity of resources and needs. Schools that have shown an embryonic interest in animal-assisted interventions, those grappling with challenges that therapy dogs could ease, and institutions that have pioneered innovative educational strategies form the nucleus of this burgeoning network. The dialogue initiated with these schools is not merely transactional but deeply exploratory, seeking to unearth shared aspirations and common grounds upon which a fruitful partnership could flourish.

22.2 Partnership Models

The architecture of these partnerships is inherently flexible, accommodating various models ranging from loosely structured alliances to formal collaborative agreements. At one end of this continuum are informal networks where schools share insights, experiences, and advice, a model that thrives on the spontaneous exchange of ideas and support. Progressing further along this spectrum, structured collaborations emerge, characterized by joint training programs, shared funding initiatives, and coordinated research endeavors. The most formalized partnerships manifest as consortia governed by agreements delineating each party's roles, responsibilities, and contributions, ensuring clarity and mutual accountability. This modular approach allows schools to navigate the terrain of collaboration that aligns with their specific circumstances and aspirations, fostering a synergy that enriches the therapy dog program and the educational community it serves.

22.3 Shared Training and Resources

Central to the vitality of this network is the pooling of training resources and expertise, a strategy that leverages the collective knowledge and capabilities of the partnership to enhance the effectiveness of therapy dog programs across schools. Joint training sessions offer a platform for exchanging best practices, innovative methodologies, and insights gleaned from the front lines of program implementation. This collaborative learning environment not only elevates the skills of handlers and educators but also fosters a sense of camaraderie among participants, strengthening the bonds within the network. Additionally, the shared development and dissemination of resources—from curricular materials to program evaluation tools—streamline efforts and reduce redundancies, ensuring that schools can access the support they need to thrive. This collective approach to training and resource development embodies the adage that the whole is greater than the sum of its parts, amplifying the impact of therapy dog programs through collaboration.

22.4 Network Support Structures

The scaffolding that supports this network consists of various structures designed to facilitate ongoing collaboration and the sharing of best practices. Online forums provide a virtual gathering space where educators, handlers, and administrators can discuss challenges, celebrate successes, and seek advice. These digital platforms are complemented by regular meetings—both virtual and in-person—that offer opportunities for more structured dialogue and planning. Specialized working groups may also be formed to address specific issues or explore new avenues for program development, drawing on the diverse expertise within the network.

Additionally, a dedicated Facebook group for school therapy teams creates a dynamic online community where members can share stories, post updates, and access resources. This group serves as a repository of knowledge and experience and a source of inspiration, highlighting the transformative power of therapy dog programs in schools.

In the efforts towards collaboration among schools, forming a network dedicated to advancing therapy dog programs transcends individual achievements, fostering a collective movement that elevates the educational experience. Schools achieve a collaboration that enriches the programs and the lives of the students they touch through carefully selecting partners, adopting flexible partnership models, pooling training resources, and establishing robust support structures. This collaborative journey, underscored by a spirit of mutual support and shared aspiration, heralds a new era in integrating therapy dogs into educational settings, paving the way for a future of enhanced student success and academic enrichment.

Chapter 23. Leveraging Media and Community Support for Expansion

In the vast landscape of educational innovation, where therapy dog programs bloom like well-tended gardens within the school ecosystems, the infusion of media and community support acts as both sunlight and rain, essential for growth and vitality. This symbiotic relationship, where each flourish of program success feeds into the community's enthusiasm and back into the program through support and recognition, forms a cycle as natural and nurturing as the earth's own.

23.1 Media Engagement

The strategy to engage media—local broadcasts, newspapers, digital platforms, and social networks—requires a thoughtful approach, similar to a botanist selecting the right conditions for rare plants to thrive. It begins with crafting stories that resonate, tales of transformation and joy brought about by the presence of therapy dogs within educational settings. These narratives, rich with the potential to touch hearts and stimulate minds, are tailored to fit the medium, ensuring that the message reaches and engages the audience. The Minnesota Video Clip, for instance, showcases Amy's non-profit "You're Not Alone" in a light that transcends the ordinary, threading the emotional connection.

In case you missed it,

YouTube clip, You're Not Alone

https://www.youtube.com/watch?v=u6Qm3dV8Bdc

Between therapy dogs and students in a narrative that captures the essence of the program's impact. This media utilization is not merely about broadcasting success; it's about inviting the community on a visual and emotional journey that illustrates the profound connections fostered by therapy dog interactions, planting the seeds of support and advocacy in fertile ground.

23.2 Community Involvement

The call for community involvement echoes through events, sponsorships, and volunteer opportunities, each an inspiration that draws individuals and organizations towards the noble cause of enriching education through therapy dog programs. Events, from fundraisers to awareness campaigns, serve as gathering points, not just for resources but for hearts and minds, rallying the community around the shared goal of student welfare. Sponsorships, whether from local businesses or more giant corporations, bring financial support and a network of potential advocates, each with the power to further the program's reach. Volunteer opportunities, crafted to invite participation in various aspects of the program, from dog training to event organization, empower individuals to contribute their skills and time, fostering a sense of ownership and commitment to the program's success. This strategy, engaging the community on multiple fronts, contributes to a more robust, more resilient support network, ensuring the program's roots in the community are deep and widespread.

23.3 Highlighting Success

The act of highlighting program success on media and community platforms transcends mere reportage; it's an art form that paints the therapy dog program in strokes broad and fine, capturing its overarching impact and the delicate moments of connection that define its essence. Success stories shared through newsletters, social media posts, and local media features, each contribute to a larger picture of transformation and healing. These carefully chosen and thoughtfully presented stories serve as testimonials to the program's efficacy, inviting the audience to witness the program's journey from inception to impact. By showcasing these successes, the program not only garners support but also inspires emulation, sparking a movement that could see therapy dog programs adopted in more schools, expanding the circle of influence and benefit.

23.4 Public Relations and Advocacy

In public relations and advocacy, the therapy dog program takes a proactive stance, leveraging media coverage and community goodwill to champion the cause of animal-assisted education. This effort, requiring both strategy and sincerity, positions the program as a beneficiary of public support and an advocate for the broader adoption of therapy dog initiatives. Through press releases highlighting groundbreaking research, op-eds arguing for policy changes, and appearances on public forums discussing educational innovation, the program amplifies its voice, reaching out to policymakers, educators, and the public with a compelling call to action.

This advocacy, grounded in the program's tangible results and emotional narratives, aims to shift perceptions and policies, promoting a future where therapy dogs are recognized not as novel but as necessary components of educational enrichment. By engaging the media for visibility, involving the community for support, showcasing successes for inspiration, and advocating for change, the therapy dog program secures its place within the educational landscape and sows the seeds for its expansion. This ensures that more students, schools, and communities can experience the unique benefits of this compassionate and transformative initiative.

Chapter 24. Future Directions: Innovations in Therapy Dog Programs

The landscape of therapy dog programs within educational settings is an ever-evolving milieu, responding with agility to students' changing needs and advancements in pedagogical and technological approaches. The horizon is dotted with emerging trends and innovations that promise to redefine the effectiveness and reach of these initiatives, ensuring their vital role in nurturing student emotional health and enhancing learning experiences.

24.1 Emerging Trends

An increasing emphasis on the holistic integration of therapy dog programs into the educational curriculum marks the vanguard of this evolution. New methodologies focus on creating seamless interactions between therapy dogs and students, where the presence of these compassionate canines is incorporated into the daily rhythm of school life. This approach extends beyond scheduled visits, embedding therapy dogs as a constant, comforting presence that students can interact with throughout their school day. Recently, the scope of these programs has been expanded to address a broader range of needs, including initiatives tailored for educators and school staff, recognizing the universal benefits of human-animal interactions.

24.2 Technology Integration

Integrating technology into therapy dog programs represents a frontier of untapped potential. For instance, virtual reality (VR) experiences are being explored to simulate interactions with therapy dogs for students in environments where live animals might not be feasible due to allergies, phobias, or logistical constraints. These VR experiences aim to replicate real-life interactions' calming and joyful effects, offering a digital bridge to the benefits of therapy dog programs. Similarly, mobile applications supporting these programs offer platforms for scheduling visits, sharing success stories, and providing educational resources on the benefits of human-animal bonds. These digital tools not only enhance the accessibility of therapy dog programs but also foster a community of practice among educators, handlers, and researchers.

24.3 Research and Development

The commitment to ongoing research and development is critical for the sustained innovation of therapy dog programs. This endeavor is like the work of scientists in a laboratory, constantly experimenting, observing, and refining their approaches to maximize outcomes. Current research focuses on quantifying the impacts of therapy dog interactions on specific educational outcomes, such as reading proficiency and math skills, while also exploring the psychological effects on student anxiety, self-esteem, and social skills. Collaborations between academic institutions and research organizations are vital, as well as pooling resources and expertise to undertake comprehensive studies that can guide the future development of therapy dog programs. This research contributes to the academic understanding of these programs' benefits and informs best practices, ensuring that programs are evidence-based and outcomes-focused.

24.4 Building a Learning Community

At the heart of these future directions is the cultivation of a vibrant learning community among schools that have embraced therapy dog programs. This community, united by a shared commitment to enhancing student well-being through animal-assisted interventions, serves as a fertile ground for exchanging ideas, challenges, and successes. Schools document their journeys by creating sample lesson plans that integrate therapy dogs and developing a repository of resources to inspire and guide new programs. Workshops and webinars offer forums for educators and handlers to share their experiences and learn from one another, fostering a culture of continuous improvement.

This learning community extends beyond schools, reaching out to parents, students, and the broader community. Inviting them to contribute their perspectives and experiences enriches the dialogue, ensuring that therapy dog programs remain responsive to the needs of all stakeholders.

In this dynamic landscape, the future of therapy dog programs in educational settings is bright, marked by a confluence of innovation, research, and community engagement. These programs are poised to continue their vital role in supporting student well-being and learning, expanding their impact by integrating new methodologies, technologies, and collaborative practices. Looking ahead, the journey of therapy dog programs is one of growth and transformation, guided by a commitment to enhancing the educational experience for all students.

As this chapter draws to a close, we reflect on the boundless potential of therapy dog programs. By embracing emerging trends and the innovative use of technology, rigorously pursuing research, and nurturing a learning community, these initiatives are set to expand their reach and deepen their impact. The journey promises discovery and enrichment as we explore new ways to integrate these compassionate canines into educational settings, enhancing the lives of students, educators, and communities alike. With eyes set on the future, we move forward, inspired by the possibilities that await in the continuing evolution of therapy dog programs.

Chapter 25: Customizing Sessions for Students with Special Educational Needs

In the context of inclusiveness, therapy dog programs emerge not as a mere embellishment but as a vital strand that strengthens the whole. Students with special educational needs represent diverse patterns, each with its own rhythm and texture. Here, in the delicate art of customizing therapy dog sessions, we find a profound opportunity for specialization and transformation.

The guiding philosophy behind this customization is simple yet profound: every student's learning journey is distinct, and their paths to growth are as varied as the patterns in a kaleidoscope. This understanding forms the foundation upon which therapy dog sessions are tailored, ensuring that these interactions transcend mere encounters and become catalysts for unlocking potential and fostering growth.

Individualized Approach

Imagine a classroom where each desk, rather than being uniform, is crafted to suit the specific needs of its occupant; some are adjustable, others equipped with specialized tools. This vision mirrors the essence of designing therapy dog sessions that cater to individualized educational plans (IEPs) for students with special educational needs. By aligning the therapeutic presence of dogs with the educational scaffolding laid out in each student's IEP, we create a bridge between two worlds. The dog becomes more than a companion; it transforms into a tool for learning, an anchor in the stormy seas of educational challenges.

Integration with Educational Goals

When a therapy dog is involved, a mathematics lesson becomes a lesson in patience and perseverance. Students struggling with complex concepts find solace in the dog's presence, a nonjudgmental companion who offers comfort amidst frustration. This scenario underscores the importance of aligning therapy dog sessions with specific educational goals. Whether reading, where the dog becomes an attentive audience, or science, where the dog's behavior sparks curiosity about the natural world, integrating therapy dogs into educational objectives enriches the learning experience, making abstract concepts tangible and approachable.

Training for Special Needs

Understanding and navigating the spectrum of special needs requires a sensitive approach in a world that often demands conformity. Training therapy dogs and their handlers to be sensitive and skilled in interacting with students across this spectrum is similar to learning a new language. It's a language of patience, subtle communication cues, and unconditional acceptance. The training involves not just the mastery of commands but the understanding of silence, the moments when a student's struggle with expression finds solace in the dog's patient presence. This training, therefore, becomes a dual journey of learning and unlearning as handlers adapt their methods to meet each student's unique needs.

Measuring Impact

In education, where outcomes and achievements are often quantified, measuring the impact of therapy dog sessions on students with special educational needs presents a unique challenge. Beyond the tangible metrics of academic performance lie the intangible benefits of emotional health, social integration, and self-esteem. Developing appropriate metrics for these sessions involves a delicate balance, capturing not just improvements in reading levels or increased classroom participation but also the smiles, moments of connection, and gradual building of confidence. These metrics, while elusive, are far from insignificant, offering a glimpse into the profound effect therapy dogs can have on students' lives.

IEP Integration

The process involves understanding a student's IEP and integrating therapy dog sessions with educational goals. It also involves training for special needs and measuring impact. The goal is to ensure that these sessions are meaningful and aligned with the broader objectives of each student's education plan.

In this chapter, the focus on individualized approaches, integration with educational goals, specialized training, and the development of detailed metrics underscores the commitment to inclusivity and personalized support that defines the use of therapy dogs in academic settings. Through careful planning, dedicated training, and a deep understanding of each student's needs, therapy dog sessions become a powerful tool in the educational toolkit, offering unique pathways to learning and growth for students with special educational needs.

Chapter 26. Cultural Sensitivity: Making Animal-Assisted Interventions Inclusive

In modern classrooms, where each student's unique heritage and worldview should be respected, the inclusion of therapy dogs enhances global connectivity. While inherently comforting, the presence of a therapy dog carries a spectrum of cultural implications, necessitating a respectful and adaptive approach.

26.1 Understanding Cultural Contexts

Navigating the cultural landscapes of students requires more than a superficial appreciation of diversity; it demands an immersive understanding. Educators and handlers are thus encouraged to embark on continuous learning, delving into the cultural backgrounds of the student body to grasp the diverse perspectives on animal-assisted interventions. This understanding is not static but evolves, reflecting the dynamic nature of culture itself. Workshops and seminars led by cultural studies experts become essential, providing platforms for educators and handlers to explore the complex relationships between culture, animals, and healing. These sessions aim to illuminate the varied cultural narratives surrounding animals, offering insight into how these beliefs might influence a student's interaction with a therapy dog. This deep dive into cultural contexts lays the groundwork for inclusive programming, ensuring that therapy dog sessions honor the diversity of student backgrounds.

26.2 Inclusive Programming

Crafting therapy dog sessions that resonate across cultural divides requires a foundational shift in programming. This shift moves beyond the mere presence of a therapy dog, integrating culturally relevant practices and symbols that acknowledge and celebrate the diversity of the student population. For instance, incorporating storytelling sessions where tales from different cultures featuring animals are shared can bridge the gap between the familiar and the novel. Such stories, accompanied by the calming presence of a therapy dog, not only enrich the session but also serve as a nod to the student's cultural heritage. Similarly, inviting students to share their stories about animals in their culture fosters a sense of belonging and recognition. This approach transforms therapy dog sessions from a universal template into a culturally sensitive experience, where respect and inclusivity pave the way for deeper connections.

26.3 Community Engagement

The awareness of cultural sensitivity in therapy dog programs is further strengthened through active engagement with parents and community leaders. This engagement is not superficial but a sincere effort to weave the insights and concerns of the community into the program's fabric. Meetings, community forums, and informal gatherings become the arenas for this engagement, offering spaces for dialogue and exchange. Here, parents and community leaders are invited to voice their perspectives on therapy dogs, sharing cultural insights that might influence the program's direction. This dialogue serves a dual purpose; it informs the program and builds a bridge of trust between the school and the community. By actively involving parents and leaders in the conversation, the program signals its commitment to cultural sensitivity, acknowledging that the success of animal-assisted interventions hinges on community support and understanding.

26.4 Adapting Practices

The true test of cultural sensitivity in therapy dog programs lies in their capacity for adaptation. Feedback and dialogue with the school community are the compass for this adaptation, guiding the program's evolution. This adaptive process may take various forms, from adjusting the timing and nature of therapy dog sessions to respect cultural holidays and observances, to modifying interaction protocols to align with cultural norms regarding animal contact. In some cases, the selection of therapy dogs may be influenced by cultural considerations, with a preference for breeds or temperaments that resonate with community preferences. This ongoing process of adaptation, grounded in feedback and open dialogue, ensures that therapy dog sessions are not only culturally sensitive but also dynamically responsive to the evolving cultural landscape of the school community.

The imperative for cultural sensitivity cannot be overstated in educational enrichment, where therapy dogs catalyze emotional and academic growth. This ensures that animal-assisted interventions are inclusive, respectful, and reflective of the diverse worldviews that populate the modern classroom. Through understanding, inclusive programming, community engagement, and adaptation, therapy dog programs affirm their commitment to honoring the cultural richness of their student body, ensuring that every child, regardless of background, finds comfort and connection in the presence of these compassionate canines.

26.5 Supporting Students with Emotional and Behavioral Challenges

Emotional and behavioral complexities benefit from the serene presence of therapy dogs. With their intuitive understanding and unconditional acceptance, these noble creatures offer unique solace and support to students navigating the turbulent waters of emotional and behavioral challenges. Designing and implementing therapy dog sessions as targeted interventions for such students is not a mere act of inclusion but a deliberate strategy to illuminate the dark corners of distress with the gentle light of companionship.

26.6 Targeted Interventions

At the heart of this strategy lies the nuanced design of

therapy dog sessions, crafted to meet each student's specific emotional and behavioral needs. This process begins with a deep dive into the individual's experiences, understanding the unique contours of their challenges, and identifying how the calming presence of a therapy dog might offer relief and reassurance. These sessions are carefully structured to create a safe space where emotions can be expressed freely, and behaviors can be observed without judgment. Within this sanctuary, the therapy dog acts as a catalyst for emotional release and behavioral adjustment, offering a physical embodiment of empathy and understanding that words alone might fail to convey. The therapeutic goals of these sessions are clear yet flexible, allowing for the natural ebb and flow of emotional states and the unpredictable journey of behavioral evolution.

26.7 Collaboration with Mental Health Professionals

The efficacy of these targeted interventions is significantly enhanced through close collaboration with mental health professionals within the school setting. School counselors and psychologists, with their deep understanding of the students' psychological landscapes, become invaluable allies in the planning and executing therapy dog sessions. This partnership allows for the seamless integration of animal-assisted interventions into students' broader mental health support plans. Together, professionals and handlers provide support that is both comprehensive and cohesive, ensuring that the therapy dog sessions complement and reinforce the therapeutic objectives set forth by the mental health team. This collaborative approach amplifies the interventions' impact. It embeds the therapy dog sessions within the context of the school's mental health framework, making them an integral part of the support system.

26.8 Crisis Intervention

The role of therapy dogs extends beyond the realm of ongoing support to become a vital component of the school's crisis intervention strategy. In moments of acute stress or upheaval, whether prompted by personal trauma or collective emergencies, the immediate presence of a therapy dog can offer a profound sense of comfort and stability. How these dogs are utilized during crises is marked by a sensitivity to the immediate emotional climate, with handlers adept at reading both the room and the moment. The therapy dog's ability to provide silent support, a physical presence that anchors and reassures, becomes invaluable in diffusing tension and alleviating distress. This intervention serves as a bridge to equilibrium, a gentle reminder of normalcy and safety amid chaos.

26.9 Building Coping Skills

Beyond the immediate relief and support offered through targeted interventions and crisis management, therapy dog sessions play a pivotal role in teaching students coping skills and resilience.

In the presence of these empathetic animals, students learn the value of patience, the strength found in vulnerability, and the power of connection. Each session becomes a practical lesson in managing emotions and navigating challenges, with the therapy dog serving as both a model and a motivator. Skills such as deep breathing, mindfulness, and emotional regulation are not merely taught but experienced, embodied in the interactions with the dog. The non-verbal communication between the student and therapy dog, rich in trust and mutual respect, lays the foundation for building resilience. These coping skills, once internalized, extend beyond the therapy dog sessions to become tools that students carry with them, a legacy of their time spent in the company of these compassionate canines.

In this focused endeavor to support students with emotional and behavioral challenges, therapy dogs emerge as companions and co-facilitators of healing and growth. These animals play a crucial role in students' emotional and behavioral development through targeted interventions, collaboration with mental health professionals, crisis intervention, and the building of coping skills. The strategy is deliberate, the implementation nuanced, and the impact profound, marking therapy dog sessions as a cornerstone of support within the educational landscape. In their silent understanding and unconditional acceptance, therapy dogs offer a lesson in empathy and resilience, guiding students toward a place of emotional stability and behavioral balance.

Chapter 27. The Role of Therapy Dogs in Crisis Situations: Best Practices

In the heart of a school community, with routine and familiarity, the unforeseen crisis cuts through like a scythe, leaving ripples of distress in its wake. Here, within this breach of normalcy, therapy dogs emerge not just as bearers of comfort but as models of stability, their presence a soft murmur of reassurance against the clamor of chaos. The orchestration of their involvement in these times of crisis demands a nuanced understanding of immediate response strategies, long-term emotional support mechanisms, handler preparedness, and post-crisis evaluations, each component a critical note in the symphony of healing.

27.1 Immediate Response

In the immediate aftermath of a crisis, whether a natural disaster tearing through the community or a traumatic event within the school's walls, the rapid deployment of therapy dog teams becomes a priority. This swift action is predicated on pre-established protocols delineating the when, where, and how of therapy dog involvement. These guidelines, developed to dovetail with the school's broader crisis response framework, ensure that introducing therapy dogs into the situation is timely and effective. It is a delicate balance to strike, where the calming presence of therapy dogs must not intrude but gently incorporate itself into the emergency response plans, offering solace without overwhelming those already grappling with shock and grief. In this scenario, the handlers act not just as guides for their canine companions but as custodians of space and comfort, their movements and decisions measured and mindful of the heightened sensitivities of the moment.

27.2 Long-term Support

Beyond the immediacy of crisis response lies the expansive terrain of long-term support, where therapy dogs play a pivotal role in the community's journey toward recovery. Here, their presence transcends the initial moments of comfort, evolving into a consistent thread of healing that extends through the following weeks and months. Integrating therapy dog sessions into the ongoing support programs offered by the school becomes a key strategy, providing students and staff with a continuity of care that aids in the gradual process of emotional restoration. These sessions, often more structured than the initial crisis response, aim to address the complex layers of trauma, offering a non-verbal form of therapy that complements traditional counseling methods. With their intuitive understanding of human emotion, the therapy dogs become silent witnesses to the stories of loss and resilience, a steady constant in the fluctuating dynamics of recovery.

27.3 Handler Preparedness

Critical to the effectiveness of therapy dogs in crises is the preparedness of their handlers, who must navigate the delicate interplay of offering support while managing their reactions to the situation. This dual challenge necessitates training beyond the standard curriculum, delving into psychological first aid and trauma-informed care. Handlers are thus equipped with the skills to support their dogs in these taxing situations and build awareness to recognize the signs of stress and vicarious trauma in themselves and their charges. This comprehensive preparation fosters an environment where the handler-dog team can function as a cohesive unit, their actions, and responses finely tuned to the needs of those they seek to support. It is a preparation that demands continuous reflection and learning, as each crisis presents unique challenges and learning opportunities.

27.4 Post-Crisis Evaluation

The shadow of a crisis looms long after the event has passed, its impact echoing in the halls of the school and the community's hearts. Within this shadow lies the opportunity for learning and growth as the school thoroughly evaluates the therapy dog program's role in the crisis response. This evaluation, rooted in both quantitative data and qualitative feedback, seeks to unravel the threads of what worked, what did not, and why. It is a reflective process where honest reflection paves the way for refining strategies and protocols. The feedback gathered from students, staff, and handlers becomes the cornerstone of this evaluation, offering insights into the efficacy of the therapy dog intervention and the areas where adjustments are needed. Through this cyclical process of action and reflection, the therapy dog program not only enhances its capacity to respond to future crises but also reinforces its commitment to the vitality of the school community.

In the scheme of a school's crisis response and recovery efforts, therapy dogs emerge as catalysts for comfort and resilience along a community's journey through trauma and healing. Their role, dynamically shifting from immediate responders to long-term supporters, underscores the nature of healing and non-verbal companionship's profound impact in navigating a crisis's aftermath. Through the reflective practice of post-crisis evaluation, therapy dog programs continue to refine their contribution to the school's crisis response, ensuring that their presence remains a source of solace and stability in the face of life's disruptions.

Chapter 28. Fostering Empathy and Social Skills: Beyond Academic Support

In the expansive realm of education, where academic excellence often takes center stage, the introduction of therapy dogs brings a unique and profound narrative that transcends traditional learning paradigms. In these nuanced interactions, students, often immersed in their own challenges and victories, discover the delicate art of empathy.

The therapy dog, with its innate understanding and non-judgmental presence, becomes a living lesson in recognizing and responding to the emotions of others. This silent curriculum, devoid of textbooks or exams, unfolds in the quiet moments of connection between student and animal, teaching empathy not through words but through the heart.

Empathy, in its purest form, is a skill honed not from solitary introspection but through the mirror of a relationship. Therapy dog sessions, therefore, are designed to foster this delicate skill among students. These sessions are not just about the presence of the dog, but also about practical exercises in emotional literacy. Students learn to interpret the subtle cues of the dog's emotions—excitement, apprehension, or contentment.

This hands-on learning approach helps students attune

themselves to non-verbal signals, a skill that extends beyond their interactions with the dog to their dealings with peers and the broader community.

Parallel to the development of empathy is enhancing social skills, a domain where therapy dog sessions excel in transforming theory into practice. The design of these sessions often encourages collaboration, inviting students to engage in tasks that require communication, negotiation, and mutual respect. Whether a group activity centered on caring for the therapy dog or a structured game involving students and the animal, the underlying goal is cultivating social skills essential for success within and beyond the school walls. In this environment, students learn the value of teamwork, the importance of clear communication, and the beauty of shared achievements, lessons that are even more resonant when discovered in the company of a therapy dog.

Creating peer interaction opportunities is another facet of therapy dog sessions that underscores their role in fostering social skills. These sessions become a nexus for students from diverse backgrounds and with varying degrees of social comfort to come together with a common purpose. The therapy dog acts as a social lubricant, easing tensions and lowering barriers that might impede interaction. As students work together to care for and learn about the therapy dog, they develop a sense of community and mutual respect that transcends the session. This collective responsibility for the support of another being teaches students about cooperation, empathy, and the shared joy of nurturing life, reinforcing the social network of the school community.

Another powerful aspect of therapy dog sessions is behavior modeling. The therapy dog's predictable and positive responses serve as a template for desirable behaviors. Students observe firsthand the outcomes of gentle handling, patience, and positive reinforcement, drawing parallels between their interactions with the dog and their behavior toward peers.

This modeling extends to emotional regulation, as the calm demeanor of a therapy dog in response to excitement or stress serves as a live demonstration of composure and resilience. Through repeated exposure to these positive behaviors and the reinforcement of similar actions in students, therapy dog sessions become a living classroom where desirable social behaviors are not only taught but also caught and internalized by students as they navigate the complexities of social interactions.

As this chapter draws to a close, empathy, and social skills emerge as vital components of a holistic educational experience. These sessions transcend the boundaries of traditional learning and offer students a unique arena where the heart is educated as much as the mind.

In the presence of therapy dogs, students learn to navigate

the emotional landscapes of themselves and others, engage in meaningful social interactions, and model behaviors that enrich their lives and those around them. Within the context of therapy dog sessions, this narrative speaks to a broader vision of education—one where the development of empathy and social skills is recognized as foundational to student success and enrichment. Your work in this area is significant and impactful, shaping the future of education.

Conclusion

Wow, what initially seemed like a relatively simple volunteer opportunity has become quite complex. After deciding to concentrate on working with schools instead of hospitals, nursing homes, or other therapeutic settings, I immediately delved more deeply into the research and real-life stories of therapy dogs in educational settings, which, along with my many years volunteering in classrooms, inspired me to write this book.

For both new therapy dog owners and seasoned school staff, the thought process of starting a therapy dog program can at first seem overwhelming. Nevertheless, do not let this stop you from beginning. From those first steps of considering the introduction of therapy dog teams into schools and wondering how to best approach school boards for approval to understanding how to measure the heartwarming impact these special dogs have on students, it can be started very simply with just one therapy dog team at a time. As we have seen, this journey is more than just about adorable dogs in classrooms; it represents a significant leap toward fostering more empathetic, inclusive, and creative educational environments.

We have unpacked the critical components needed for the successful integration of therapy dogs—from comprehending their profound impact to navigating the legal waters and getting our furry and human teammates ready for the nitty-gritty of running and assessing the results. Each piece of this puzzle is vital for creating a program that not only exists but thrives, touching lives and hearts for many years.

The benefits? Oh, they are undeniable. We have delved into the research and shared stories showing how much of a positive force these therapy dog teams can be. It is not just the students who benefit—the whole school community, from the faculty to the student's families and sponsors; everyone gets to share this joy. It is a collective experience that binds us all, fostering a sense of connection and community that is truly special.

Success in this endeavor is a collaborative mission. It is about our mutual sense of purpose—passionate teachers, students, parents, and administrators—coming together with open hearts and minds. It is about embracing new ideas, keeping the lines of communication wide open, sharing ideas, and being resourceful. Remember, starting with just one or two volunteer teams can spark significant change without costing much money or taxing existing school staff.

So, what is next? I urge you – yes, you who are reading this – to take a step toward bringing a therapy dog program to your local school, no matter how small. Advocate for these programs, share the stories and evidence we have discussed, and become a catalyst for change in your community.

Consider joining the terrific private Facebook group "School Therapy Dogs." Some members have personalized trading cards describing their therapy dogs and including pictures, which they then share with other therapy dog teams nationwide, like pen-pals. Mac and I will be starting this immediately to leave behind a tangible reminder of our visits and network with others in this endeavor. These cards serve as a memento of the love and comfort the therapy dogs and their handlers share at schools.

In this Facebook group, I also found Kate Miller & Shiloh Dailey's Colorado State University School of Social Work, "Animal-Assisted Therapy Curriculum for Schools, A Collaborative Guide for School Professionals and HABIC Volunteers in School Placements, Fall 2023. "

Animal-assisted interventions are ever-evolving, and staying curious and adaptable is vital. Something new is always on the horizon – new research, legal guidelines, and best practices. Let us commit to being lifelong learners in this endeavor.

On a personal note, I am filled with hope and excitement for the future of therapy dog programs in schools everywhere. My vision? A world where every school has access to such a program, making schools a more compassionate and supportive atmosphere for all students. Alongside Mac, my faithful companion, I am committed to continuing this adventure, aiming to bring you more stories of success and learning in the years to come. While the shortage of health professionals continues, volunteer therapy dog teams in schools can be a practical and cost-effective way to help our students in so many positive ways.

Thank you for your interest and dedication to exploring the world of therapy dog teams in schools. Your curiosity and willingness to embrace this idea can genuinely make a difference in facilitating more nurturing and supportive educational atmospheres.

To those who have walked this path with Mac and me, providing guidance, support, and the wisdom we needed to have confidence in our mission, thank you from the bottom of my heart. Your contributions have been instrumental in this book and the evolution of Mac and me as a successful team.

Remember, if you volunteer, your presence and support in schools can make a difference, even if you decide not to become a therapy dog team volunteer. A little bit of your time can light up a student's world, offering them the encouragement and strength they need to succeed.

As we look forward to publishing this summer and hope more schools can welcome therapy dog teams in the 2024-2025 academic year, I invite you to join this growing community of compassionate, dedicated individuals. Whether bringing your trained dog friend into the classroom or simply lending a hand as an individual, your contributions can be invaluable. Let us make our schools a haven of comfort, learning, empathy, and joy together.

Thank you for being part of this journey, and once again, thank you to the professionals committed to this cause. Here is to making a difference, one paw print at a time!

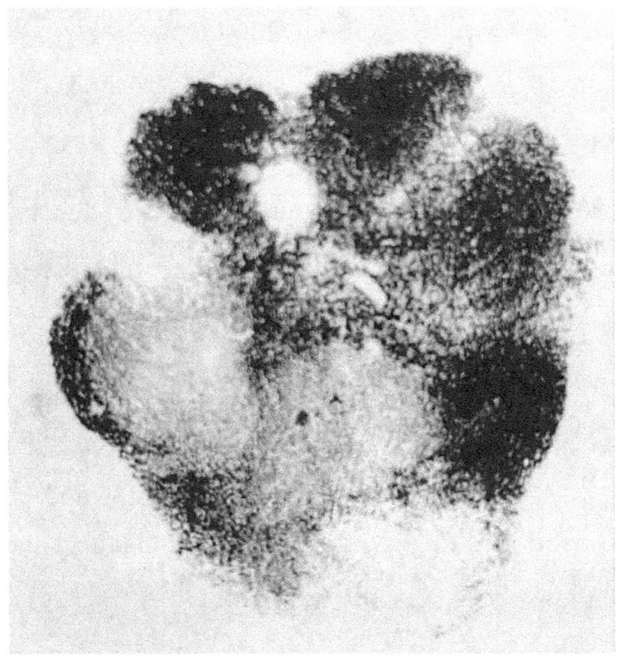

Footnote

Since I began writing this book, the school session for most counties has ended. This summer, Mac and I started working with our public library youth program to continue with his training within student environments. Twice a week, we meet and greet children from toddlers to teenagers, introducing therapy dogs before public reading times. It is gratifying when some of the same children come back, specifically to visit with Mac.

When I first approached our library, they felt they needed more information to approve our visits. After further discussions and explaining that our certifying organization, Alliance of Therapy Dogs, provided insurance for VOLUNTEERS, the staff agreed to try utilizing therapy dogs in conjunction with their summer youth activities. We are still finding the best ways to achieve our goals, but Mac is overjoyed to go to the library. That is the actual test of a successful therapy dog! Loving their job!

Also, recently, regarding the well-being of our youth, a statement from the U.S. Surgeon General was released stating:

"The mental health crisis among young people is an emergency - and social media has emerged as an important contributor. Adolescents who spend more than three hours a day on social media face double the risk of anxiety and depression symptoms, and the average daily use in this age group, as of the summer of 2023, was 4.8 hours."

Vivek H. Murthy, U.S. Surgeon General

So, in addition to schools, more parents and communities can advocate for library programs, where students will have safe spaces for less media and more community programs with face-to-face activities and opportunities to socialize in person with peers.

Latest Data From NIHCM, July 9, 2024

Across the country, nearly 20% of youth under 17 years old have a mental, emotional, developmental, or behavioral disorder.

The rate of mental health conditions among this age group has been increasing dramatically in recent years.

Addressing child and adolescent mental health is essential to achieving positive, overall well-being. Click below for the infographic:

https://nihcm.org/publications/building-strong-foundations-childrens-mental-health

Thanks, Dana, Chris, and Rachel, for helping me reach the finish line!

Please Help Spread the Word With Your Book Review. Scan the QR Code Below for print versions of the book, or click on the Direct Link Below for electronic versions to Leave Your Review!

Title: 'Implementing Therapy Dog Teams in Partnership with Best Practices for Schools: An Introduction for Volunteer Dog Handlers, Teachers, Counselors, and Administrators for Successful Integration Resulting in Researched Enhanced Student Well-Being'

Welcome to the book review page for 'Implementing Therapy Dog Teams in Partnership with Best Practices for Schools,' – a groundbreaking book that explores the benefits of implementing therapy dogs in schools to enhance student well-being worldwide. In this new book, Gabrielle Matthew sheds light on the transformative power of therapy dogs in educational settings. By incorporating these remarkable animals into schools, we can create nurturing environments that positively impact entire school communities – including staff, students, and administrators. From reducing stress and anxiety to increasing motivation and engagement, these furry friends offer a unique and valuable form of support as well as the potential for improved academic performance.

Through heartwarming stories, scientific research, and practical advice, 'Implementing Therapy Dog Teams in Partnership with Schools' aims to inspire and educate readers about the extraordinary potential of therapy dogs in schools. By leaving a review for this book, you not only become an advocate for helping to spread the message but also contribute to the expansion of these programs worldwide. Your review can make a significant difference.

https://www.amazon.com/dp/B0DBWKMFWG

The positive reviews received here will serve as testimonials, encouraging administrators and policymakers to consider implementing therapy dog programs in their educational institutions and encouraging more volunteers to train therapy dogs. Let your voice be heard and make a difference in the lives of countless students and school communities.

Thank you for considering leaving a review for 'Implementing Therapy Dog Teams in Partnership with Best Practices for Schools.' Your review can profoundly impact the lives of students, dog handlers, and school communities worldwide. We appreciate your time and effort in sharing your thoughts, personal experiences, and the impact therapy dogs have had on your life or the lives of others. Please click on the direct link or scan the QR code above to leave your review.

Therapy Dog References

ABC Action News. (2022a, April 8). Therapy dogs helping school-age children [Video]. YouTube. https://www.youtube.com/watch?v=bsWJvP0Cr8U

American Kennel Club. (n.d.-a). Canine Good Citizen (CGC) – American Kennel Club. https://www.akc.org/products-services/training-programs/canine-good-citizen/

American Kennel Club. (n.d.-b). CGC Test Items – American Kennel Club. https://www.akc.org/products-services/training-programs/canine-good-citizen/canine-good-citizen-test-items/

Amvettergmailcom. (2022, December 7). Collaborations between Teachers and Therapy Dog Teams: Increasing Children's Writing Skills and Inspiring Them for Life. Writers Who Care. https://writerswhocare.wordpress.com/2022/12/05/collaborations-between-teachers-and-therapy-dog-teams-increasing-childrens-writing-skills-and-inspiring-them-for-life/

Australia, T. D. (n.d.). Therapy Dogs Australia. https://therapydog.com.au

Baird, R., Berger, E., & Grové, C. (2023a). Therapy dogs and school well-being: A qualitative study. Journal of Veterinary Behavior,68, 15–23. https://doi.org/10.1016/j.jveb.2023.08.005

Baird, R., Grové, C., & Berger, E. (2022a). The impact of therapy dogs on the social and emotional well-being of students: a systematic review. The Educational and Developmental Psychologist, 39(2), 180–208. https://doi.org/10.1080/20590776.2022.2049444

Blad, E. (2023a, January 24). Using Therapy Dogs in Schools: 8 Do's and Don'ts. Education Week. https://www.edweek.org/leadership/using-therapy-dogs-in-schools-8-dos-and-donts/2023/01

Blad, E. (2023b, February 7). Gone to the Dogs? Schools Use Therapy Animals to Boost Mental Health, Academics. Education Week. https://www.edweek.org/leadership/gone-to-the-dogs-schools-use-therapy-animals-to-boost-mental-health-academics/2023/01

Brelsford, V., Meints, K., Gee, N., & Pfeffer, K. (2017). Animal-Assisted Interventions in the Classroom—A Systematic Review. International Journal of Environmental Research and Public Health/International Journal of Environmental Research and Public Health,14(7), 669. https://doi.org/10.3390/ijerph14070669

Cairns, H. (2023a, March 16). The Benefits of Therapy Dogs in Students' Mental Health and in Schools? College Raptor. https://www.collegeraptor.com/find-colleges/articles/student-life/benefits-of-therapy-dogs-in-school/

Calzon, B. (2023a, August 10). What is data analysis? Methods, techniques, types & how-to. B.I. Blog | Data Visualization & Analytics Blog | Datapine. https://www.datapine.com/blog/data-analysis-methods-and-techniques/

Carmel Goes to School: Vokatis, Barbara, Kiskis, Halina: 9781962765008: Amazon.com: Books. (n.d.). https://www.amazon.com/Carmel-Goes-School-Barbara-Vokatis/dp/1962765008/ref=sr_1_3?crid=3A3TH4I10URWV&dib=eyJ2IjoiMSJ9.NrVpIIK6beerROaH7reiVr-sS2RStdjTsO2Pc3YbA7ppYDsB6idvdi7qoT9-UR1Gceka8shvA_NK8491-sPAhg.rZZ6PW4PktanQ7UTGB46n7NKHk8HNYAUGl-di2pfljI&dib_tag=se&keywords=carmel+therapy+dog&qid=1710715812&s=books&sprefix=carmel+therapy+dog%2Cstripbooks%2C88&sr=1-3

ConnectAd. (2023, February 10). 5 Reasons for Therapy Dog Certification with ATD. Alliance of Therapy Dogs Inc.

https://www.therapydogs.com/5-reasons-for-therapy-dog-certification-with-atd/?gad_source=1&gclid=CjwKCAiArLyuBhA7EiwA-qo80BZFoA8OKRZ5d2AhnNx1Mv_XVWC4GG-v4hPEJwK3AfdV7wkQ-K9nWxoC708QAvD_BwE

Dalien, L. (2023, September 13). Animal Therapy For Children With Special Needs. Special Ed Resource. https://specialedresource.com/animal-therapy-children-special-needs/

December 2022 – Writers Who Care. (n.d.). Writers Who Care. https://writerswhocare.wordpress.com/2022/12/

Dogs, A. O. T. (2022, July 7). How do Therapy Dogs Help in the Classroom? - Alliance of Therapy Dogs Inc. Alliance of Therapy Dogs Inc. https://www.therapydogs.com/how-do-therapy-dogs-help-in-the-classroom/

First-of-its-kind risk assessment tool ensures the highest standards for animal-assisted interventions in schools | WALTHAM. (n.d.). https://www.waltham.com/news-events/safe-animal-assisted-interventions-schools

Frsc, S. C. P. D. (2020, June 4). A tiny Yorkshire Terrier may have been the first recognized therapy dog. Psychology Today. https://www.psychologytoday.com/us/blog/canine-corner/202006/who-was-the-first-therapy-dog

Frsc, S. C. P. D. (2023a, November 1). Studies on the effectiveness of therapy dogs have tested mostly females to date. Psychology Today. https://www.psychologytoday.com/us/blog/canine-corner/202311/therapy-dogs-comfort-regardless-of-gender-or-sexual-identity

Gee, N. R., Rodriguez, K. E., Fine, A. H., & Trammell, J. P. (2021). Dogs Supporting Human Health and Well-Being: A Biopsychosocial Approach. Frontiers in Veterinary Science, 8. https://doi.org/10.3389/fvets.2021.630465

Gibson, A. (2023, May 17). The Healing Power of Dogs - CASSY. CASSY - Counseling & Support Services for Youth. https://cassybayarea.org/the-healing-power-of-dogs/

Glenk, L. M. (2017). Current Perspectives on Therapy Dog Welfare in Animal-Assisted Interventions. Animals, 7(12), 7. https://doi.org/10.3390/ani7020007

Grové, C., Henderson, L., Lee, F., & Wardlaw, P. (2021a). Therapy Dogs in Educational Settings: Guidelines and Recommendations for Implementation. Frontiers in Veterinary Science, 8. https://doi.org/10.3389/fvets.2021.655104

Home. (n.d.-a). My Vxw Site Icqgxx. https://www.schooltherapydogs.org/

Human-Animal Bond Research Institute. (2020a, March 5). HABRI | The Human Animal Bond Research Institute. HABRI. https://habri.org/?gad_source=1&gclid=CjwKCAjw4f6zBh BVEiwATEHFVoYrqtQc0AxfhL20R7t3_Mk4074rRftlwA CZfWA71zCpPZJYisOHhhoC13QQAvD_BwE

James, D. (2023, June 19). Mom's mission to bring therapy dogs to Minnesota schools is taking off. CBS News. https://www.cbsnews.com/minnesota/news/moms-mission-to-bring-therapy-dogs-to-minnesota-schools-is-taking-off/

Ketter, K. (2023, July 5). Pet Partners and The Pet Care Trust: Dogs in the Classroom Program. Pet Partners. https://petpartners.org/pet-partners-and-the-pet-care-trust-dogs-in-the-classroom-program/

Kropp, J. J., Ph. D, CCLS, Shupp, M. M., BBA, Georgia Southern University, & College of Business. (2017). Review of the Research: Are Therapy Dogs in Classrooms Beneficial? In Forum on Public Policy. https://files.eric.ed.gov/fulltext/EJ1173578.pdf

Kunz, J. (2019, July 10). How Pet Therapy Helps Kids with Special Needs - St. Mary's Kids. St. Mary's Kids. https://www.stmaryskids.org/how-pet-therapy-helps-kids-with-special-needs/

Lesté-Lasserre, C. (2023, September 27). Therapy dogs in
classrooms may improve children's well-being. New
Scientist. https://www.newscientist.com/article/2393986-
therapy-dogs-in-classrooms-may-improve-childrens-well-
being/

McDowall, S., Hazel, S. J., Cobb, M., & Hamilton-Bruce, A.
(2023). Understanding the Role of Therapy Dogs in Human
Health Promotion. International Journal of
Environmental Research and Public Health/International
Journal of Environmental Research and Public Health,
20(10), 5801. https://doi.org/10.3390/ijerph20105801

Meixner, J., & Kotrschal, K. (2022). Animal-Assisted
Interventions With Dogs in Special Education—A
Systematic Review. Frontiers in Psychology, 13.
https://doi.org/10.3389/fpsyg.2022.876290

Millward, E. (2020, April 23). More schools are choosing therapy
dogs, even with an uncertain school year ahead. WCPO 9
Cincinnati. https://www.wcpo.com/news/local-news/more-
schools-are-choosing-therapy-dogs-even-with-an-
uncertain-school-year-ahead

Must love dogs movie - Google Search. (n.d.).
https://www.google.com/search?q=must+love+dogs+movie
&oq=must+love+dogs+mo&gs_lcrp=EgZjaHJvbWUqCgg

AEAAY4wIYgAQyCggAEAAY4wIYgAQyBwgBEC4Yg
AQyBggCEEUYOTIHCAMQABiABDIHCAQQABiABD
IHCAUQABiABDIHCAYQABiABDIHCAcQABiABDIH
CAgQABiABDIHCAkQABiABKgCALACAA&sourceid=
chrome&ie=UTF-8

Napolitano, J. (2023a, January 24). 6 Ways Therapy Dogs in
Schools Help Students Succeed. Puppington.
https://puppington.co/blogs/pup-wellness/6-ways-therapy-
dogs-in-schools-improve-mood-performance-and-quality-
of-life-to-help-students-succeed

Navolio, M. (2024, February 23). Strategies for Successful K-12
Survey Design and Analysis. Hanover Research.
https://www.hanoverresearch.com/insights-blog/k-12-
education/strategies-for-successful-k-12-survey-design-
and-analysis/?org=k-12-
education&tm=tt&ap=gads&aaid=adaFTiRMzQBWb&kw
=&cpn=20960886423&utm_term=&utm_campaign=k12-
general&utm_source=adwords&utm_medium=display&hs
a_acc=3558395466&hsa_cam=20960886423&hsa_grp=&h
sa_ad=&hsa_src=x&hsa_tgt=&hsa_kw=&hsa_mt=&hsa_n
et=adwords&hsa_ver=3&gad_source=1&gclid=CjwKCAj
w4f6zBhBVEiwATEHFVnROUBDFSyARa0sWs6kH6_Q
TEucl1_wZtpEs0ee0C0bsq2mJ_JKKzxoCLGAQAvD_Bw
E

Oregonian/OregonLive, S. S. |. (2020, January 30). Archie, a therapy dog, has a full-time job at Portland's Franklin High School (Video). Oregonlive.https://www.oregonlive.com/education/2020/01/archie-a-therapy-dog-has-a-full-time-job-at-portlands-franklin-high-school-video.html

Peel, N., Nguyen, K., & Tannous, C. (2023). The Impact of Campus-Based Therapy Dogs on the Mood and Affect of University Students. International Journal of Environmental Research and Public Health/International Journal of Environmental Research and Public Health, 20(6), 4759. https://doi.org/10.3390/ijerph20064759

Pet allergy - Diagnosis & treatment - Mayo Clinic. (2021a, August 4). Mayo Clinic. https://www.mayoclinic.org/diseases-conditions/pet-allergy/diagnosis-treatment/drc-20352198

Pets in the Classroom. (2024, June 27). Education Grant for Teachers - Pets in the Classroom. Education Grants | Pets in the classroom Is an Educational Grant Program to Support Public School Teachers to Have Aquarium Fish or Small Pets in the classroom. https://petsintheclassroom.org/?gad_source=1&gclid=CjwKCAjw4f6zBhBVEiwATEHFVrIIjRiyXAVpTM1FdYnEp=

we24etMB7LqrwJ3P40NtKKv_7MzPLo7BoCyUMQAvD_BwE

Piper, G. (2024a, April 15). Therapy Dogs in Schools: Vet-Verified Benefits, Uses & FAQ – Dogster. Dogster. https://www.dogster.com/lifestyle/therapy-dogs-in-schools

Portell, M. (n.d.). Therapy dogs changed the culture of mental health in this Central Valley district [edsource.org]. PACEsConnection. https://www.pacesconnection.com/blog/therapy-dogs-changed-the-culture-of-mental-health-in-this-central-valley-district-edsource-org

Pros and Cons of Therapy Dogs in Schools - EducationalWave. (2024, April 7). EducationalWave - Pros and Cons Explained. https://www.educationalwave.com/pros-and-cons-of-therapy-dogs-in-schools/

Rowan, L. (2023a, April 28). Why therapy dogs are gaining popularity on college campuses. Cardinal News. https://cardinalnews.org/2023/04/28/therapy-dogs-are-gaining-popularity-on-college-campuses/

Sager, S. (2023a, January 19). Therapy dogs help young students develop reading skills at Nassau County School. ABC7 New York. https://abc7ny.com/therapy-dog-reading-long-island-school/12719113/

Schools Programme Discovery Video. (n.d.). [Video].

https://paws-therapydogs.com/schools/

Serpell, J. A., Kruger, K. A., Freeman, L. M., Griffin, J. A., & Ng, Z. Y. (2020a). Current Standards and Practices Within the Therapy Dog Industry: Results of a Representative Survey of United States Therapy Dog Organizations. Frontiers in Veterinary Science, p. 7.

https://doi.org/10.3389/fvets.2020.00035

Service Animals & Therapy Dogs at School | Thrun Law. (n.d.).

https://www.thrunlaw.com/news/service-animals-therapy-dogs-school

Sheade, H., & Chandler, C. K. (2019a). Cultural Diversity Considerations in Animal Assisted Counseling. ResearchGate.

https://www.researchgate.net/publication/335681618_Cultural_Diversity_Considerations_in_Animal_Assisted_Counseling

Steel, J. (2022). Children's well-being and reading engagement: the impact of reading to dogs in a Scottish Primary one classroom. Education 3-13, 1–16.

https://doi.org/10.1080/03004279.2022.2100442

Teich, D. (2023, November 28). Therapy dogs in schools: What exactly do they do? ManyPets.

https://manypets.com/us/blog/therapy-dogs-in-schools/

Therapy Dog Grants - CHBF. (n.d.-a). CHBF.
https://charlottehelenbaconfoundation.org/programs/therap
y-dog-grants/

Therapy Dog Programs: Improving Student and Staff Well-Being.
(2023a, December 13). NASSP.
https://www.nassp.org/2021/03/16/therapy-dog-programs-
improving-student-and-staff-well-being/

Therapy Dog Writing Activities. (n.d.). TPT.
https://www.teacherspayteachers.com/Product/Therapy-
Dog-Writing-Activities-8017285

Therapy dogs encourage NYC elementary school students to read
with an adorable program. (2023, May 31). ABC7 New
York. https://abc7ny.com/therapy-dogs-reading-
elementary-school-in/13324817/

Therapy dogs enhance learning for young children. (n.d.). College
of Education and Human Ecology.
https://ehe.osu.edu/news/listing/therapy-dogs-enhance-
learning-young-children

Therapy Dogs Help Reduce Students' Anxiety and Stress and
Bring Smiles to DCSD Students and Staff. (n.d.-a).
https://www.dcsdk12.org/about/our_district/news/therapy_

dogs_help_reduce_students__anxiety

Therapy Dogs Help Students Cope with Trauma, Reduce Stress, Anxiety and Improve School Attendance. (n.d.). https://nned.net/947/

Valiyamattam, G., Yamamoto, M., Fanucchi, L., & Wang, F. (2018). Multicultural Considerations in Animal-Assisted Intervention. Human-Animal Interactions Bulletin. https://doi.org/10.1079/hai.2018.0019

Verhoeven, R., Butter, R., Martens, R., & Enders-Slegers, M. (2023). Animal-Assisted Education: Exploratory Research on the Positive Impact of Dogs on Behavioral and Emotional Outcomes of Elementary School Students. Children, 10(8), 1316. https://doi.org/10.3390/children10081316

VonLintel, J., B.F. Kitchen Elementary School, Bruneau, L., & Adams State University. (n.d.-a). Pathways for Implementing a School Therapy Dog Program: Steps for Success and Best Practice Considerations. Abstract, 2. http://www.jsc.montana.edu/articles/v19n14.pdf

WCCO - CBS Minnesota. (2023, June 19). School in session for these therapy dogs [Video]. YouTube. https://www.youtube.com/watch?v=u6Qm3dV8Bdc

WCPO 9. (2020a, April 23). More schools are choosing therapy dogs, even with an uncertain school year ahead [Video]. YouTube. https://www.youtube.com/watch?v=RAifuS1lkxg

We Are Head Over Tails in Love With Wisconsin's School Support Dogs. (2023, May 9). Wisconsin Department of Public Instruction. https://dpi.wi.gov/news/dpi-connected/wisconsins-school-support-dogs-are-very-good-dogs-indeed

Wheeler, L. (2022, May 11). 4 Legged SEL: How to Start a Therapy Dog Program. Edutopia. https://www.edutopia.org/article/4-legged-sel-how-start-therapy-dog-program/

Whitfield, J. & Northrop Grumman Health Solutions. (2005). Successful Strategies for Recruiting, Training, and Utilizing Volunteers: A Guide for Faith- and Community-Based Service Providers. In Center for Substance Abuse Treatment. Substance Abuse and Mental Health Services Administration. https://www.samhsa.gov/sites/default/files/volunteer_handbook.pdf

Wintermantel, L., & Grove, C. (2022). An evaluation of a dog-assisted social and emotional learning intervention in a school setting: Study protocol for a cluster-randomized trial. Mental Health & Prevention, 28, 200246. https://doi.org/10.1016/j.mhp.2022.200246

WUSA9. (2023, February 3). Therapy dog helps students with special needs in Virginia [Video]. YouTube. https://www.youtube.com/watch?v=eacgjEUNxr0

Kjellstrand, J. (2024). Animal-assisted school counseling. Routledge Taylor & Francis Group.

Health References

Abrams, Z. (n.d.). Kids' mental health is in crisis. Here's what psychologists are doing to help. https://www.apa.org. https://www.apa.org/monitor/2023/01/trends-improving-youth-mental-health

Abramson, A. (n.d.). Children's mental health is in crisis. https://www.apa.org. https://www.apa.org/monitor/2022/01/special-childrens-mental-health

Agency for Healthcare Research and Quality (U.S.). (2022, October 1). CHILD AND ADOLESCENT MENTAL HEALTH. 2022 National Healthcare Quality and Disparities Report - NCBI Bookshelf. https://www.ncbi.nlm.nih.gov/books/NBK587174/

Building strong foundations: children's mental health. (n.d.). NIHCM. https://nihcm.org/publications/building-strong-foundations-childrens-mental-health

Child and Adolescent Mental Health Outcomes Are Declining Despite Continued Improvements in Well-being Indicators - Child Trends. (n.d.-a). ChildTrends. https://www.childtrends.org/publications/child-and-adolescent-mental-health-outcomes-are-declining-despite-continued-improvements-in-well-being-indicators

England, N. (2023, November 21). NHS England: » One in five children and young people had a probable mental disorder in 2023. https://www.england.nhs.uk/2023/11/one-in-five-children-and-young-people-had-a-probable-mental-disorder-in-2023/

Mental Health. (n.d.). DASH | CDC. https://www.cdc.gov/healthyyouth/mental-health/index.htm

National Alliance on Mental Illness. (2024, May 16). Mental Health By the Numbers | NAMI. NAMI. https://www.nami.org/about-mental-illness/mental-health-by-the-numbers/

Office of the Assistant Secretary for Health (OASH). (2023, May 23). Surgeon General Issues New Advisory About Effects Social Media Use Has on Youth Mental Health. HHS.gov. https://www.hhs.gov/about/news/2023/05/23/surgeon-general-issues-new-advisory-about-effects-social-media-use-has-youth-mental-health.html

Quick Facts and Statistics About Mental Health. (n.d.). Mental Health America. https://mhanational.org/mentalhealthfacts

Search. (n.d.). ChildTrends. https://www.childtrends.org/search?s=mental+health&_gl=

1*mw45l5*_up*MQ..&gclid=CjwKCAjw4f6zBhBVEiwA

TEHFVk_IMOYNlu6i5BzrCbY8w5Plp3V3v1q4iGD_XIN

arWGHTlSSrQITNxoCcI8QAvD_BwE

Warren, D. (2024, June 26). The State of Pediatric Mental Health
in America 2023 Report. Office Practicum.
https://www.officepracticum.com/blog/the-state-of-
pediatric-mental-health-in-america-2023-report/

World Health Organization: WHO. (2021, November 17). Mental
health of adolescents. https://www.who.int/news-room/fact-
sheets/detail/adolescent-mental-health

Youth data 2022. (n.d.). Mental Health America.
https://www.mhanational.org/issues/2022/mental-health-
america-youth-data

Book Summary

Explore the transformative potential of therapy dogs in enhancing student well-being and inclusivity with 'Implementing Therapy Dog Teams in Partnership with Schools.' This comprehensive guide offers proven strategies for cost-effectively integrating therapy dog teams (trained and certified dogs together with their human handler partners) into educational settings, resulting in a more positive and engaging learning experience for all students.

It is more than just theory – it is actionable advice backed by sound research and successful real-life case studies. Therapy dogs have proven beneficial in creatively improving students' mental health, academic performance, peer relationships, and social skills. The presence of therapy dogs in schools has been linked to enhanced mood, confidence, self-esteem, and overall life satisfaction among students. Additionally, these partnership teams have been shown to improve children's self-regulation behavior, making the classroom environment more conducive to learning. This heightened interest in learning has also resulted in reduced absenteeism as well as a greater sense of belonging within the school community.

Our youth increasingly suffer from various emotional health and learning challenges. This resource guide provides practical advice on how to best select, utilize, and evaluate the positive contributions that therapy dogs bring to schools. It breaks down all your questions into manageable sections, explicitly outlined in the table of contents.

Ready to make a difference? Embrace this innovative strategy that promises heart-warming, remarkable results, bridging connections for entire school communities. Whether you are an educator, dog trainer, or volunteer, this book equips you to create more vibrant learning environments with multifaceted adaptations that can work anywhere, anytime, for any student, given appropriate collaborations with school staff and administration.

Join my mini-sheepadoodle dog, Mac, and me on this impactful journey!

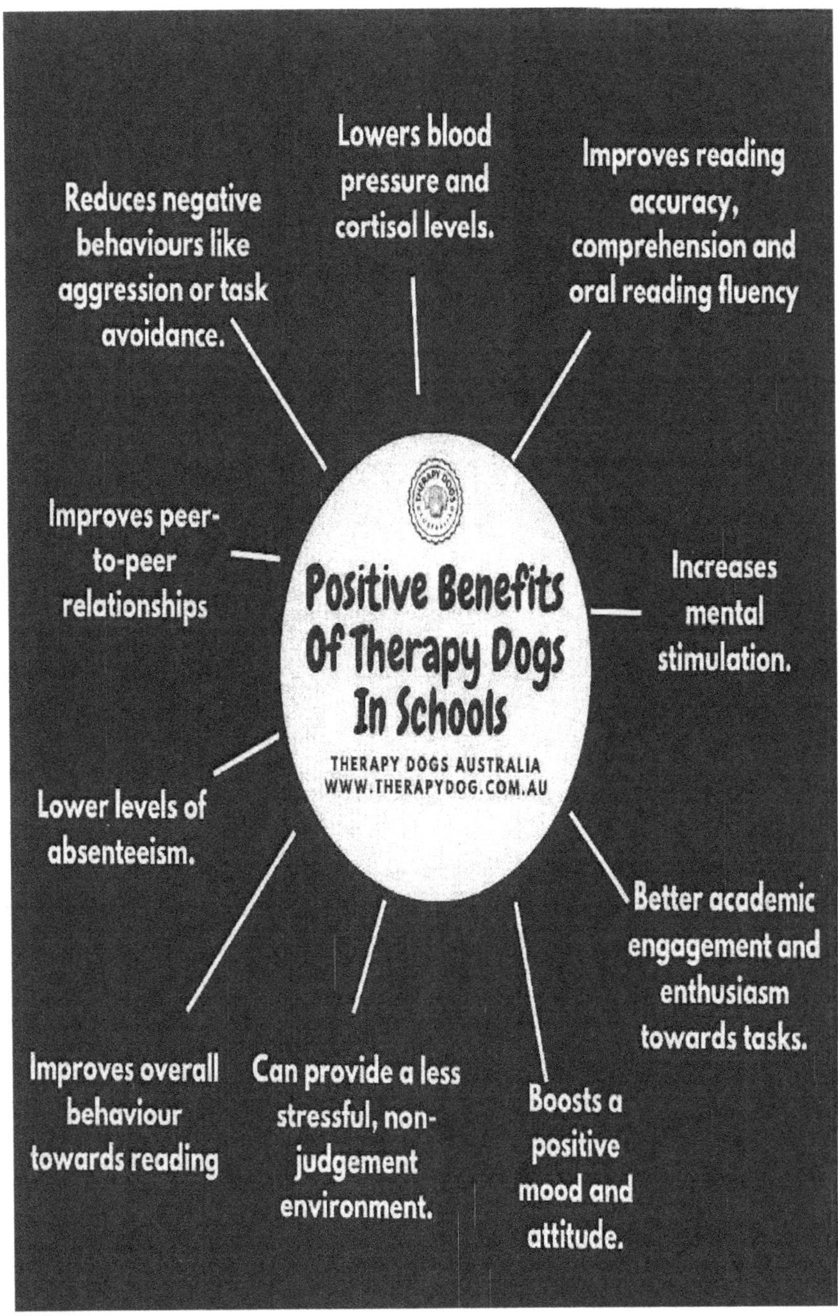

Lowers blood pressure and cortisol levels.
Reduces negative behaviours like aggression or task avoidance.
Improves reading accuracy, comprehension and oral reading fluency
Improves peer-to-peer relationships
Positive Benefits Of Therapy Dogs In Schools
THERAPY DOGS AUSTRALIA
WWW.THERAPYDOG.COM.AU
Increases mental stimulation.
Lower levels of absenteeism.
Better academic engagement and enthusiasm towards tasks.
Improves overall behaviour towards reading
Can provide a less stressful, non-judgement environment.
Boosts a positive mood and attitude.